Spirit to Spirit

THE MYSTERIES OF CONNECTING TO THE HEAVENLY OF HEAVENS

Dr. Y. Bur

Available Titles

ASITPLEASESGOD.COM

SPIRIT TO SPIRIT

THE MYSTERIES OF CONNECTING TO THE HEAVENLY OF HEAVENS

Copyright © 2021 by R.O.A.R. Publishing Group. All rights reserved.

Visit www.RoarPublishingGroup.com for more information. No part of this publication may be reproduced, stored in a retrieval system, or transmitted in any way by any means, electronic, mechanical, photocopy, recording, or otherwise, without the prior permission of the author, except as provided by USA copyright law.

R.O.A.R. Publishing Group
581 N. Park Ave. Ste. #725
Apopka, FL 32704
ROAR-58-2316
762-758-2316
www.RoarPublishingGroup.com

Send Questions or Comments to:
CustomerService@RoarPublishingGroup.com

Published in the United States of America
ISBN: 978-1-948936-51-4
$22.88

Please Send Prayers, Testimonies, Donations, or Orders To:

Dr. Y. Bur
R.O.A.R. Publishing Group
581 N. Park Ave. Ste. #725
Apopka, FL 32704
ROAR-58-2316
762-758-2316

✉ Dr.YBur@gmail.com

Visit Us At:

📷 AsItPleasesGodMovement
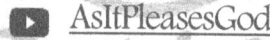 AsItPleasesGod

 DrYBur.com
 AsItPleasesGod.com

Please Donate

Please DONATE to this *Missionable Movement of God* as a GIVE-BACK to the Kingdom. Thanks for your support. Many Blessings.

AIPG Donation Link

Scan to Pay

Table of Contents

Introduction	7
Chapter One	11
Stomping Ground	11
Chapter Two	17
Enough is Enough	17
Chapter Three	23
Spiritual Tutor	23
Chapter Four	37
Spirit to Spirit	37
Chapter Five	47
Redeeming The Times	47
Chapter Six	55
Lifestyles of the Ancient	55
Chapter Seven	75
Grandfather Clause	75
Chapter Eight	87
In Him	87
Chapter Nine	97
Perceptional Worthiness	97
Chapter Ten	111
Heavenly Perspective	111

Chapter Eleven 125
    Fullness Therein 125
Chapter Twelve 131
    As it Pleases God 131

INTRODUCTION

The Spiritual Journey of Healing is a predestined factor we will all endure, but we should not do it alone. We need help without being left to our own devices, especially when we are fragile, weak, or off-keeled. Most often, we do not tap into this Divine Reservoir because we do not understand 'What' to do, 'How' to do it, 'Where' to tap in, 'When' to do so, 'Why' we should, and with 'Whom.' Above all, if we have a desire to achieve and do more in the Kingdom, we must tap into the *Spirit to Spirit* Connection from the Heavenly of Heavens, aligning with our Divine Blueprint.

The motivational factors embedded in our DNA either spark or deflate our enthusiasm in or out of the Kingdom of God, causing some to run toward or away from Religion. In contrast, the goal of *Spirit to Spirit* is to bring us into a Relational Oneness *In Him.* In order to capitalize on our Blessings or Birthrights, this is not something we try out for a day, and if it does not work, we move on. It is a developmental process similar to a parent-child relationship.

Often enough, we get a lot of hoopla about who is right or wrong, while it is a distraction causing us to fight among ourselves, distorting our *Perceptional Worthiness.* However, all hope is not lost. The *Grandfather Clause* is designed to open the Spiritual Veil, allowing our Spiritual Eyes to See, our Spiritual Ears to Hear, and our Spiritual Language to sound its Divine Voice in the Heavenly of Heavens as we enter our *Stomping Ground* of Divine Purpose.

According to the Ancient of Days, when we have an explanation of 'What' we should do and 'Why,' we are better able to understand

and implement the *How To* process and then outright Lead by Example while becoming stronger, wiser, and consistent with our Heaven on Earth Experience. In this Spiritual Connection, this Book, *Spirit to Spirit*, is designed to change the trajectory of our lives while empowering us with the Spiritual Tools, confidence, and know-how needed to say, '*Enough is Enough*' to the Vicissitudes of Life.

As Kingdom Inspiration avails itself, it comes with *Spiritual Tutors* for the journey ahead; therefore, we cannot develop a deaf ear to the information, lessons, or whatever is designed to assist in *Redeeming the Times* on our behalf or that of another. Amid all, on this narrow path, there are two factors hidden in plain sight:

1. We have the power to positively or negatively ENCOURAGE ourselves and others.

2. We have the power to positively or negatively DISCOURAGE ourselves and others.

In a *Spirit to Spirit* Relationship, memorizing scripture does not seal the Spiritual Oneness desired from the Heavenly of Heavens to know the difference between these two factors. We need the Holy Spirit involved to know the actual difference in what we are or are not doing as it relates to our ability to encourage or discourage.

According to the Kingdom, it is the Relational Aspects and Spiritual Principles with applied scripture that place a Spiritual Seal on whatever, however, or with whomever. The bottom line is that saying one thing and doing another are two totally different actions; therefore, we must rely on the Word of God that is written on the Tablet of the Heart while wholeheartedly being in the Will of God. To be clear, knowing and memorizing the Word of God is good, but if we are not incorporating the Fruits of the Spirit and using Christlike Character, our memory alone cannot and will not bring stability and balance to our Earthen Vessels.

As It Pleases God: Book Series

As a Word to the Wise, *Spirit to Spirit*, we should not allow the ability NOT to remember something to stop us from doing what we are called to do, especially when we are GIFTED with the ability to document whatever with whomever. Besides, the Mind of a Genius is not set on remembering what can be documented; it is set on RECEIVING what most refuse to document!

Listen, when dealing with the *Fullness Therein*, if the heart is not leading us to do the right thing, regardless of how much we proclaim righteousness, sugarcoat our lives, or what we are going through, the conscience requires Spiritual Training. We need a *Spirit to Spirit* Relationship to recall, recalibrate, and restore the human psyche according to the Principles and Standards of the Kingdom continuously. If not, we will function at a limited capacity, overlooking the hidden Gifts of Greatness from within, not realizing the mind must be decluttered to receive Spiritual Downloads from the Kingdom above, *As It Pleases God*.

Now, from a *Heavenly Perspective*, we are all important in the Eye of God. He will always have our best interests at heart. So, if we dare to tap into the Greatness He has already placed within us, He will not disappoint, guaranteed. Even if we have to work harder before we become smarter, it is entirely okay. It has taken me many years to get to this point, but it has been well worth it, especially when I can reach back to help another person walk in their Divine Purpose. More importantly, each one of us will have the same ability to unveil our Greatest Potential without having to settle for mediocrity or a cycle of déjà vu.

The *Lifestyle of the Ancient* of Days has provided a glimpse into how we must conduct ourselves on a moment-by-moment basis, including our behaviors behind closed doors or when no one is looking. Most would think a *Spirit to Spirit* Connection is limiting, but it is totally the opposite. Actually, it is more liberating than we could ever imagine, giving us Spiritual Leverage beyond what we could ever envision on our own and bringing forth the Hidden Treasures from within. The moment we release ourselves from a self-induced coma or lethargy, we will find our Gift of Greatness making room for us, setting us before men in high places.

As It Pleases God: Book Series

Regardless of where you are, what you are going through, or what you are doing in life, I want to take a moment to say, 'I believe in you.' So, if you are ready to get the ball rolling with the Second Book of the '*As It Pleases God*' Book Collection, let us do this together, *Spirit to Spirit*.

Chapter One

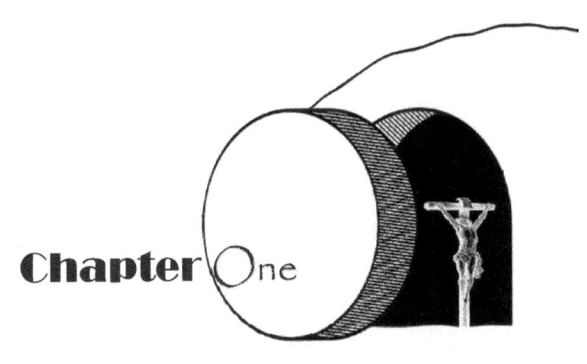

STOMPING GROUND

When entering into being in Purpose on purpose, we have a uniqueness about us that is displayed by Divine Default. This pristineness is similar to having a certain glow or aura about us that is noticeable, yet may not be understood by those not possessing the Holy Spirit or who have not polished up their Spiritual Instincts or Discernment. When dealing with our Gifts, Calling, Talents, and Creativity, we all have something to *'Give Back'* to the Kingdom of Heaven as a token of appreciation. However, we may not all know what it is, and for this reason, in this chapter, the goal is to help narrow this down, ensuring we develop a clear image of our Divine Blueprint or *Stomping Ground*, which is already.

What is our *Stomping Ground?* It is a place of many Blessings relating to being in Purpose on purpose, using our Gifts, Calling, Talents, and Creativity to build and edify the Kingdom of God. When we are rooted in the Divine Abundance of God, no one can stop His Divine Overflow, nor can they thwart His Mission.

On the other hand, if or when we get off course, we do not want to run to God to have a pity party, especially if we are dead set on doing what we want to please ourselves. Understandably, we all have issues in need of reckoning, but we should not wait until the last minute to work on them. We can block or delay our Blessings, preparation, or training. Plus, we do not want to be ill-prepared when evilness attacks us from the inside out, and then we try to play cleanup when the Wrath of God is upon us. In my opinion, this is similar to King Saul's experience in 1 Samuel 16, where the Spirit of God departs from him, and something evil torments his psyche to no avail.

We often run into a brick wall, suffering multiple failures and setbacks due to some form of disobedience relating to the hidden elements of selfishness intertwined in our senses, habits, or lusts. What causes this to happen? It will vary from person to person; however, it could be due to a few things, but not limited to such:

1. We have the wrong motives with our Gifts, Calling, Talents, or Creativity, causing us to manipulate, scheme, bully, or use others.
2. We follow the vision of another as it relates to our Gifts, Calling, Talents, or Creativity, causing us to shy away from our Divine Blueprint just to feel accepted, fit in, or prove our loyalty.
3. We are not passionate about our Gifts, Calling, Talents, or Creativity, contributing to greediness, ungratefulness, or laziness.
4. We are trying to recreate the wheel of our Gifts, Calling, Talents, or Creativity based upon some form of superficial worldly expectations.
5. We are negative or doubtful about our Gifts, Calling, Talents, or Creativity while NOT creating a win-win out of everything or developing a Positive Mental Mindset.
6. We have not taken the time to mind-map or journal the instructions or pointers given about our Gifts, Calling, Talents, or Creativity, only to find ourselves wandering in circles without a Plan of Action.
7. We are not learning, growing, and sowing back into the Kingdom as it relates to our Gifts, Calling, Talents, or

As It Pleases God: Book Series

Creativity, as if we were self-created. And, from my perspective, had it not been for God's GRACE and MERCY, we would not be where we are today.

8. We are consumed Mentally, Physically, Emotionally, and Spiritually with jealousy, envy, pride, and coveting, blocking access to our Gifts, Calling, Talents, or Creativity.
9. We are exhibiting competitiveness, causing all forms of disobedience and uncooperativeness in the conveyance of our Gifts, Calling, Talents, or Creativity.
10. We are oblivious to exhibiting the Fruits of the Spirit or Christlike Character, perfecting our People Skills.
11. We are operating in an unrepenting or unrelenting Spirit.
12. We have not involved the Holy Trinity in our Gifts, Calling, Talents, or Creativity.

How do we know when we are on our *Stomping Ground*? Our inner man will know, mainly when our Spiritual Instincts are heightened. What does this mean? *Spirit* knows *Spirit*, and if we become One with the Holy Spirit and covered by the Blood of Jesus, we will know. Here is what the scripture says about the noticeable indications of being on our *Stomping Ground*: "*Then the Spirit of the LORD will come upon you, and you will prophesy with them and be turned into another man. And let it be, when these signs come to you, that you do as the occasion demands; for God is with you.*" 1 Samuel 10:6-7. Amid all, once this happens, we must step up to the plate to take possession of our Gifts, Calling, Talents, Creativity, or Birthright.

What is the purpose of taking possession of what is already? First, God will not violate our free will. Secondly, if we develop a deaf ear to Him, becoming disobedient, the Mantle can pass to the next in line, similar to the anointing of David as the next King after the downfall of King Saul. Let us align this accordingly, "*So, he sent and brought him in. Now he was ruddy, with bright eyes, and good-looking. And the LORD said, 'Arise, anoint him; for this is the one!'* Then Samuel took the horn of oil and anointed him in the midst of his brothers; and the Spirit of the

As It Pleases God®: Book Series

LORD came upon David from that day forward. So, Samuel arose and went to Ramah." 1 Samuel 16:12-13.

How can our *Stomping Ground* benefit us when the Spirit of the Lord comes upon us? Once again, we are all different; therefore, it will vary from person to person, circumstance to circumstance, region to region, condition to condition, and so on. When it comes down to the Kingdom, we are not an overnight sensation; we must be trained, equipped, tested, and commissioned. In the Eye of God, what works for one person may not necessarily work for another. Yet, listed below are a few profound BENEFITS to embrace:

1. We will experience placement growth, becoming fruitful from the inside out.
2. We will experience a peaceful rest beyond human understanding.
3. We will have access to Supernatural Wisdom, gaining access to the Secrets, Mysteries, and Principles of the Kingdom to create a Divine Flow.
4. We will have Divine Understanding, keeping us 'In The Spiritual Know.'
5. We will have the Spirit of Counsel, guiding and advising on all things Spiritual and earthly.
6. We will have the Spirit of Knowledge that is teaching, training, and strengthening us on a moment-by-moment basis.
7. We will have a fearful reverence of God, keeping us humble, respectful, repenting, and prayerful.

Here is the scripture to align some of the *Stomping Ground* benefits: *"There shall come forth a Rod from the stem of Jesse, and a Branch shall grow out of his roots. The Spirit of the LORD shall rest upon Him, the Spirit of Wisdom and Understanding, the Spirit of Counsel and Might, The Spirit of knowledge and of the fear of the LORD."* Isaiah 11:1-2. What is the purpose of these benefits? They will help to avoid bringing shame to our names and the Kingdom while polishing our Fruits of the Spirit and Christlike Character to create excellent *People Skills*.

When taking possession of our *Stomping Ground*, it is imperative to make sure we are rooted and grounded in righteousness. When bearing fruit, it gives birth to our Tree of Life. On the other hand, if we are bringing forth bad fruits, we become tied to the Tree of Death until the generational curse is lifted, reversed, or broken. How do we know the difference? It is noticed in our character traits and fruits.

With all due respect, it does not take a rocket scientist to simply pay attention. Often enough, we know what and who we are dealing with, but we are in denial because we do not want to know or deal with the truth. What are the indications of the *Tree of Life*? Listed below are a few indications, but not limited to such:

1. When the Spirit of God is upon us.
2. When the Anointing of God permeates our lives.
3. When we can share the Word of God with no strings attached, without being ashamed of the Gospel, and not beating others over the head with it.
4. When we can share the Goodness of God, building up those who are down.
5. When we are humble in our approach to healing the brokenhearted, wounded, and abandoned.
6. When we can share the Freedom of the Kingdom, along with the free will liberations we are all entitled to.
7. When we make Spiritual Decrees that carry weight in the Kingdom.
8. When we do not seek revenge on those who do not believe, while remaining kind, compassionate, understanding, and exhibiting Christlike Character.
9. When we share the Fruits of the Spirit with all we come in contact with.
10. When we can reverse negative outcomes into a win-win, while keeping a Positive Mental Mindset.

11. When we give thanks and praise to God for all things, even when we cannot have our way.
12. When we grow and sow back into the Kingdom, bearing much fruit in the Spirit of Righteousness, ensuring God is glorified.

In putting all things into their proper perspective, here is the scripture we need to know when praying for, ushering in, or regrafting our *Tree of Life*. "*The Spirit of the Lord GOD is upon Me, Because the LORD has anointed Me to preach good tidings to the poor; He has sent Me to heal the brokenhearted, to proclaim liberty to the captives, and the opening of the prison to those who are bound; to proclaim the acceptable year of the LORD, and the day of vengeance of our God; to comfort all who mourn, to console those who mourn in Zion, to give them beauty for ashes, the oil of joy for mourning, the garment of praise for the spirit of heaviness; that they may be called trees of righteousness, the planting of the LORD, that He may be glorified.*" Isaiah 61:1-3.

Once we come into Oneness with the Holy of Holies on our *Stomping Ground*, it symbolically becomes Holy as well. How so? Unbeknown to most, when operating in the Spirit of Righteousness, God will fight for us. To obtain this Divine Privilege, we cannot fight evil with evil; we must fight evil with good, especially if we want justification for all of our good deeds.

Spiritual Interdependence on a Divine Level is the way to go when dealing with the enemy's wiles. With Divine Leverage as such, when they play dirty, we can say, *Enough is Enough* while playing cleanly with the Spirit of the Lord on our side, without becoming shady, evil, or rude. Here is what to recite in our *Spirit to Spirit* Communal Time with God Almighty: "*Through You we will push down our enemies; through Your name we will trample those who rise up against us. For I will not trust in my bow, nor shall my sword save me. But You have saved us from our enemies, and have put to shame those who hated us.*" Psalm 44:5-7.

Chapter Two

ENOUGH IS ENOUGH

Is anything ever enough for us? When do we draw the line in the sand with our ungratefulness? Or better yet, when will we deal with the quicksand hidden in our psyche? The sinking feeling that nothing is enough has a grip on our Divine Destiny, sucking the life out of it, out of us, and anyone we come in contact with. More importantly, if we do not gird up our loins to do something about it, it will disappear under layers of debris into the elements of the unseen.

Unbeknown to most, those who are ungrateful most often do not realize they are. Once we become accustomed to this characteristic, it causes us to adapt to its conditions. What does this mean? When ungratefulness becomes our norm, our psyche will block our conscience from alerting us to any form of unappreciativeness. As a result of this negative oversight, our psyche sucks in the negativity as a form of nutrition, feeding, nurturing, and growing until it snowballs into a full-blown case of worldly materialism at its best. Then, once we are consumed, we pass this negative character trait into our Bloodline, not realizing the manifestation is growing bigger and bigger as time passes.

As It Pleases God®: Book Series

When we talk about ungratefulness, it has a wide range of attributes leading up to a downfall or building up for an eruption of our Bloodline. In so many words, ungratefulness becomes like a plague, consuming all who are in our path without us realizing it. Frankly, this plague is so silently potent to the point where we do not even realize we generate it. As a matter of fact, we will think everyone else has the issue without ever once thinking to examine ourselves.

Well, dear heart, the buck stops here! We must regraft this negative character trait, keeping us bound to not appreciating the simple things in life, such as Love, Joy, Peace, Patience, Kindness, Goodness, Faithfulness, Gentleness, and Self-Control. Why do we need them, especially when they are not putting food on the table? In my opinion, they help to keep food on the table Mentally, Physically, Emotionally, and Spiritually. Plus, they keep us from getting caught up in a web of deception based on our overzealous wants, needs, and desires, or outright selling our souls for material things. Moreover, they help us combat jealousy, envy, pride, coveting, and competitiveness that lead to all other forms of inner debauchery and rotten fruits.

As we take this a step further, negative characteristics contaminate the food we bring to the table on any level and with anyone. How is this possible, especially when we are Believers? No one is exempt from the effects of negativity, nor are we exempt from becoming a victim unless it is counteracted with positivity and gratefulness.

When our lives become fed with hate, misery, chaos, unkindness, rudeness, deceit, harshness, and recklessness, we inadvertently become susceptible to the Gravitational Pull of ungratefulness. This is why the Bible says, "*Do not eat the bread of a miser, nor desire his delicacies; for as he thinks in his heart, so is he. 'Eat and drink!' he says to you, but his heart is not with you. The morsel you have eaten, you will vomit up, and waste your pleasant words.*" Proverbs 23:6-8. For the most part, we think life is all fun and games, and we should overlook certain things as long as we get what we want; yet, when we become ensnared, then we are left to wander how it happened. Well, this is how it happens; we ignore the Nuggets of Wisdom and red flags forewarning us about things to come based on certain character traits or defects.

What is the big deal about character? Our character is who we are from the inside out, and regardless of whether we are negatively flawed or positively enhanced, it will manifest outwardly in due time. Moreover, here is why it is so crucial for us to say, *Enough is Enough* on ungratefulness, *"For the wrath of God is revealed from heaven against all ungodliness and unrighteousness of men, who suppress the truth in unrighteousness, because what may be known of God is manifest in them, for God has shown it to them. For since the creation of the world His invisible attributes are clearly seen, being understood by the things that are made, even His eternal power and Godhead, so that they are without excuse, because, although they knew God, they did not glorify Him as God, nor were thankful, but became futile in their thoughts, and their foolish hearts were darkened."* Romans 1:18-21.

According to the Heavenly of Heavens, we must work on ourselves consistently to become better, wiser, and more astute, taking the higher road of Spiritual Redemption. What does this mean? We are able to be kind to others amid their debaucherous efforts without expecting to get something out of it. Here is a scripture breaking ungratefulness to the core: *"But love your enemies, do good, and lend, hoping for nothing in return; and your reward will be great, and you will be sons of the Most High. For He is kind to the unthankful and evil. Therefore, be merciful, just as your Father also is merciful."* Luke 6:35-36.

To be clear, the act of doing good starts as an inner manifestation first, making itself outward. Just because we are merciful does not mean we have to subject ourselves to provocation or abuse. What does this mean? There are times we must love, forgive, and have mercy while pleading the 5th or peacefully walking away with clean hands and a pure heart. What is the purpose of doing so? Our job is to exhibit the Fruits of the Spirit and Christlike Character, not to wallow or entertain the *Gravitational Pull* of rotten fruits.

When used as a Vessel of God, we must do what we are called to do and keep it moving. Believe it or not, negativity feeds upon positivity for temporary energy, similar to a solar panel. Once we feel the drain or the zap of energy, we need to back up or move on, period! Plus, when the Holy Spirit leads us, we will receive instinctual nudges when to hold, fold, or walk away, but we must be Spiritually Awake to receive.

Unbeknown to most, we are confusing staying WOKE with being Spiritually AWAKE. Here is the deal: Woke is in reference to worldly things based upon human perception, biases, conditioning, and so on, with a specific target in mind. Meanwhile, being Spiritually Awake or Woke is derived from our Spiritual Instincts back by the UNCTION of the Holy Spirit, dealing with our psyche and spreading outwardly.

When being Spiritually Awake or Woke, we must understand our *What, When, Where, Why, How,* and with *Whom* self-analysis first, ensuring our outer manifestations are in alignment with building the Kingdom, the Fruits of the Spirit, and Christlike Character. Unfortunately, it is not based upon tearing down, belittling, disrespecting, or pointing the finger; it is predicated on becoming Spiritually Aware of what God is expecting from us regarding our Heaven on Earth Experience.

How do we know if we are consumed with ungratefulness? First, it appears in our relationship with God, ourselves, and others, in this order. Secondly, it is evident in our thoughts, character, words, deeds, demeanor, behaviors, and so on. Thirdly, it is also determined by the *Gravitational Pull* of whatever is spinning our cycle or who is stimulating or attempting to defrag our Divine Blueprint, positively or negatively.

2 Timothy 3:1-7 says, *"But know this, that in the last days perilous times will come: For men will be lovers of themselves, lovers of money, boasters, proud, blasphemers, disobedient to parents, unthankful, unholy, unloving, unforgiving, slanderers, without self-control, brutal, despisers of good, traitors, headstrong, haughty, lovers of pleasure rather than lovers of God, having a form of godliness but denying its power. And from such people turn away! For of this sort are those who creep into households and make captives of gullible women loaded down with sins, led away by various lusts, always learning and never able to come to*

the knowledge of the truth." However, if we are plagued by this now, all hope is not lost; therefore, let us go deeper.

Gratefulness helps us REPENT and create a win-win out of everything, regardless of how it appears to the naked eye. The goal is to focus our energy on the Eye of God, bringing forth the Fruits of the Spirit while exhibiting Christlike Character to all we come in contact with. Does it work? Of course, I am living proof. Plus, it enhances our *People Skills* to a level the enemy cannot contend with. Here is the *Spiritual Seal* bridging the gap to all, *"But I say to you, love your enemies, bless those who curse you, do good to those who hate you, and pray for those who spitefully use you and persecute you, that you may be sons of your Father in heaven; for He makes His sun rise on the evil and on the good, and sends rain on the just and on the unjust."* Matthew 5:44-45.

God is the Creator of it all, and if we operate in the Spirit of Righteousness, He will make all things work for our good, especially when the Spirit of Love is involved. What is the benefit of loving those who hate, use, abuse, or despise us? It helps us maintain the bonds of love within our human psyche, preventing an uprising from within and allowing us to help ourselves and others proactively.

In the Kingdom, it does not benefit us to hate, abuse, misuse, or engage in debauched behaviors. Instead, it creates Spiritual Taboos and generational curses; therefore, it behooves us to use the Fruits of the Spirit to change the trajectory of our Bloodline, especially if we have fallen short. According to scripture, it says, *"But above all these things put on love, which is the bond of perfection. And let the peace of God rule in your hearts, to which also you were called in one body; and be thankful. Let the word of Christ dwell in you richly in all wisdom, teaching and admonishing one another in psalms and hymns and spiritual songs, singing with grace in your hearts to the Lord. And whatever you do in word or deed, do all in the name of the Lord Jesus, giving thanks to God the Father through Him."* Colossians 3:14-17.

Spirit to Spirit, there is no need to player-hate or second-guess ourselves or others. The goal is to become thankful in all things while creating a win-win by reversing our negatives into positives through our words, affirmations, scriptures, behaviors, thoughts, and so on. So, get out of the quicksand, *Enough is Enough*, and step up to your rightful place in the Kingdom. "*For in it the righteousness of God is revealed from faith to faith; as it is written, 'The just shall live by faith.'* " Romans 1:17.

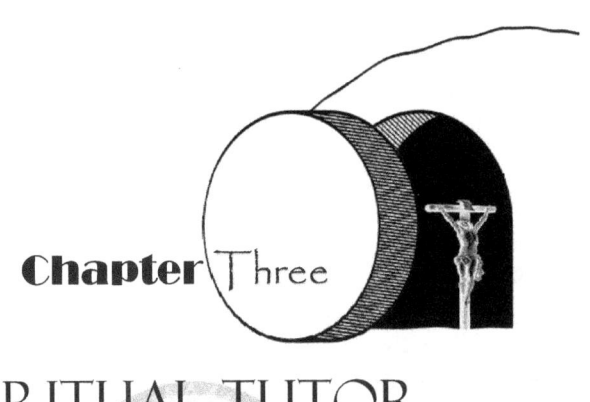

Chapter Three

SPIRITUAL TUTOR

Spiritual Tutoring is not often spoken about from a *Spirit to Spirit* perspective. The goal of this chapter is to maneuver through life with the Holy Trinity, the Fruits of the Spirit, and our Christlike Character as our Weapons of Warfare and our Hidden Advantage. How is this possible when the beatdown from the inside out is so real? In all reality, we have the last say, especially if we know 'What' we are saying, 'Why' we are saying it, 'How' to say whatever, 'Where' to say what is ailing us, 'When' to say our Divine Decrees, and with 'Whom.'

Why do we need a *Spirit to Spirit* encounter? It helps us to become AWARE of a specific condition in our psyche that has the potential to drive us senseless, especially if we become worldly without having a *Spiritual Tutor* to reel us in, Mentally, Physically, or Emotionally. Here is what we need to know about this condition: *"Behold, the days are coming, says the Lord GOD, that I will send a famine on the land, not a famine of bread, nor a thirst for water, but of hearing the words of the LORD. They shall wander from sea to sea, and from north to east; they shall run to and fro, seeking the word of the LORD, but shall not find it. In that day the fair virgins and strong young men shall faint from thirst."* Amos 8:11-13.

As It Pleases God®: Book Series

Who is our *Spiritual Tutor*? The Holy Spirit is our *Spiritual Tutor*; however, we must first develop a Spiritual Relationship with the Holy Trinity (The Father, Son, and Holy Spirit). He is a package deal. If not, we can engage in a Spirit of a different kind, which is unholy or dark in nature. Therefore, we must be specific, and for this book, we are only dealing with the Heavenly of Heavens and the Kingdom of God, to bring our Earthen Vessels into the LIGHT.

When embarking upon a *Spirit to Spirit* Relationship, we do not have to memorize scripture; we simply need to know where to gain access to it. Why do we need to know this? Most people shy away from reading or understanding the Word of God because they cannot remember it or how to access scripture. However, on behalf of the Heavenly of Heavens, it is okay not to remember, as long as we are willing to use the Word of God as a Spiritual Compass and document accordingly. What does this mean? In the same way that we Google everything else, positively or negatively, we are able to Google scriptures as well. It is perfectly okay to research scriptures, especially when it comes down to our Salvation.

In the Kingdom, it is not about what we know; it is about how well we listen, *Spirit to Spirit*. And whether or not we are documenting what we know and what is given to us *Spirit to Spirit* to refer back to, or share when the time is right.

To be clear, Google cannot save us, nor is it a ticket into Heaven, but it is a tool helping us to help ourselves, cross-reference what we do not understand, or pinpoint the Promises of God. Therefore, it behooves us to use it to Decree the Decreeable or Denounce the Denounceable while our *Spiritual Tutor* trains us in Kingdom Protocols and Principles. Listed below are a few Spiritual Decrees to preface our prayer with, but not limited to such:

1. We must avoid deceitfulness within ourselves and others, or indulging in deceitful measures, while redirecting all things toward righteousness in prayer, using our inside or outside voice. What does this mean? We do not need to be heard while sending up a justifiable prayer amid whatever or whomever. All we need to do is make sure we are not

praying amiss, intimidating others, lying to ourselves, or behaving pompously. Here is the Spiritual Decree to preface our prayer, "*Hear a just cause, O LORD, attend to my cry; give ear to my prayer which is not from deceitful lips.*" Psalm 17:1.

2. We must avoid seeking revenge, allowing God to take the wheel regarding any form of injustice while redirecting our focus to the positive, productive, and fruitful. Here is the Spiritual Decree to preface our prayer, "*Let my vindication come from Your presence; let Your eyes look on the things that are upright.*" Psalm 17:2.

3. We must set a guard over our mouths at all times, exercising great caution about what we are speaking over ourselves and others on a moment-by-moment basis. How is this possible? It is developed through having our *Mindset* locked on doing and becoming righteous in all things, knowing we are being watched. Here is the Spiritual Decree to preface our prayer, "*You have tested my heart; You have visited me in the night; You have tried me and have found nothing; I have purposed that my mouth shall not transgress. Concerning the works of men, By the word of Your lips, I have kept away from the paths of the destroyer.*" Psalm 17:3-4.

4. We must stay on course with the Blueprint set forth by the Heavenly of Heavens without having all types of distractions causing us to lose focus, jump the track with negativity, or our psyche to become further traumatized. What if we do not know the Blueprint? Then, it is best to get rid of the distractions, set aside some alone time, and focus while developing a Mind Map of the desires of the heart and awakening our Spirit to become One with the Holy Spirit. Here is the Spiritual Decree to preface our prayer, "*Uphold my steps in Your paths, that my footsteps may not slip.*" Psalm 17:5.

5. We must communicate with God in a *Spirit to Spirit Connection*. How do we go about doing so? The same way we speak to our parents, siblings, friends, husband, wife, children, or whomever, we must communicate as such, but with much reverential respect, involving the Holy Trinity in Unison. Here is the Spiritual Decree to preface our prayer, "*I have called upon You, for You will hear me, O God; incline Your ear to me, and hear my speech.*" Psalm 17:6.

6. We must ask for revelation when we are unclear, confused, lack understanding, under attack, and so on. Here is the Spiritual Decree to preface our prayer, "*Show Your marvelous lovingkindness by Your right hand, O You who save those who trust in You From those who rise up against them.*" Psalm 17:7.

7. We must ask for Divine Covering. Should we not already have it, especially if we are Believers? Of course, we have a covering to a certain extent, but we must also realize we have free will, and the Spirit cannot violate our will in certain areas. Therefore, we must learn how to invoke the Heavenly of Heavens at the drop of a dime without crying wolf. Here is the Spiritual Decree to preface our prayer, "*Keep me as the apple of Your eye; hide me under the shadow of Your wings, from the wicked who oppress me, from my deadly enemies who surround me.*" Psalm 17:8-9.

8. We must become aware of our environment and the people we hang around with. Most often, we become ensnared because we ignore the fruits, especially the loudest person in the room and those who prey upon the weak, vulnerable, and wounded. Here is the Spiritual Decree to preface our prayer, "*They have closed up their fat hearts; with their mouths they speak proudly. They have now surrounded us in our steps; they have set their eyes, crouching down to the earth, as a lion is eager to tear his prey, and like a young lion lurking in secret places. Arise, O LORD, confront*

him, cast him down; deliver my life from the wicked with Your sword." Psalm 17:10-13.

9. We must be willing to come boldly to the Throne of God, asking for what rightly belongs to us and being satisfied without becoming jealous, envious, greedy, or covetous. It is not wise to have anyone or anything unlike or contradicts the Kingdom. Here is the Spiritual Decree to preface our prayer, *"With Your hand from men, O LORD, from men of the world who have their portion in this life, and whose belly You fill with Your hidden treasure. They are satisfied with children, and leave the rest of their possession for their babes. As for me, I will see Your face in righteousness; I shall be satisfied when I awake in Your likeness."* Psalm 17:14-15.

10. We must love the Lord with all our hearts without attempting to use or pimp Him for the Benefits of the Kingdom. We need Kingdom Benefactors who receive Blessings to Bless another, keeping the Heavenly Provisions flowing, and contributing to our Heaven on Earth Experience. Here is the Spiritual Decree to preface our prayer, *"I will love You, O LORD, my strength. The LORD is my rock and my fortress and my deliverer; my God, my strength, in whom I will trust; my shield and the horn of my salvation, my stronghold."* Psalm 18:1-2.

11. We must praise God for who He is, not for what He does for us. Blasphemy, right? Wrong. Most often, we interchange praise as a form of thanks without initially giving or saying thanks at all. Whereas in the Kingdom, praise is praise, and giving thanks is just that. Therefore, amid our praises, we should NOT forget to give thanks. It keeps ungratefulness from settling in our psyche. Plus, settled ungratefulness keeps us focused on the negative and blinded to the positive or win-win. For this reason, we must become thankful for all things while learning the necessary lessons; even if it

hurts, something does not appear as we hoped, we have fallen short, and so on. Furthermore, it keeps us from praising on the one hand and hating our life on the other.

Unsettled feelings get swept under the rug all the time. But for me, I am here to pull the rug from under this deceptive measure that is thwarting our walk with God. Here is the Spiritual Decree to preface our prayer, *"I will call upon the LORD, who is worthy to be praised; so shall I be saved from my enemies."* Psalm 18:3. *"He delivers me from my enemies. You also lift me up above those who rise against me; You have delivered me from the violent man. Therefore, I will give thanks to You, O LORD, among the Gentiles, and sing praises to Your name. Great deliverance He gives to His king, and shows mercy to His anointed, to David and his descendants forevermore."* Psalm 18:48.

12. We must make our best attempts to keep our hands clean without playing dirty, cleansing our souls continuously. Psalms 19:12 says, *"Who can understand his errors? Cleanse me from secret faults."* Here is the Spiritual Decree to preface our prayer, *"Therefore the LORD has recompensed me according to my righteousness, according to the cleanness of my hands in His sight."* Psalm 18:24.

What is a Spiritual Decree? It means we have the right to quote scripture back to God as Spiritual Leverage, especially if we are in alignment with it to the best of our ability, understanding, or Spiritual Level. And once decreed, the Holy Spirit will do the rest, especially if we are using the Fruits of the Spirit and exhibiting Christlike Character. What is considered doing the rest for us as Believers? We are all different. The correction I would need will not be the same for another person. Due to our differences, God is gracious and merciful, allowing the Holy Spirit to help us along the way as a *Spiritual Tutor*.

As It Pleases God: Book Series

When dealing with all things Spiritual, we cannot pretend to be an amateur when we are a Spiritual Elite, and we cannot pretend to be a Spiritual Elite when we know we are still in the Milking Stages. Why can we not name it and claim it? The Sword of the Spirit is not something we want to play around with; therefore, it is best to humble ourselves in the Ways of God and repent at the drop of a dime. How is this possible, especially when we are being tried to the fullest? Although every situation or circumstance is different in the Eye of God, varying from person to person. Nonetheless, here is what I would say when I do not understand, lack full details, or when I need to glean information, *"Let the words of my mouth and the meditation of my heart be acceptable in Your sight, O LORD, my strength and my Redeemer."* Psalm 19:14.

When we use our *Spiritual Tutor*, we can indeed depend on Spiritual Wisdom instead of our own sense of wisdom, shifting us from a worldly perspective to a Kingdom one. What is the purpose of doing so? Our Divine Blueprint is equipped with the Spiritual Tools we need to succeed, regardless of how it may appear to the naked eye.

What is more, if we allow the Leading of the Spirit to guide us, we will not miss the mark, especially if we make it our business to do everything in the Spirit of Excellence while using the Fruits of the Spirit and Christlike Character as our Weapon of Warfare. How do we maximize our Weapons in the face of our enemies?

1. We must become understanding and compassionate toward others.
2. We must avoid becoming arrogant, biased, or condescending. Unbeknown to most, humility is our true power.
3. We must avoid chaos, deflecting it toward the positive or outright removing ourselves from the environment.
4. We must NOT become a know-it-all or the loudest person in the room. Remember, we are all on a learning curve in some area, and we gain more by effectively listening to

become *In-The-Know* than by constantly responding in irrelevancy.
5. We must govern what comes out of our mouths, choosing our words carefully.
6. We must not seek revenge, squashing the enemy from within while invoking the Genius or Giant that is at our beck and call.
7. We must think, behave, and become positive.
8. We must seek peace in all things, especially from the inside out, while learning how to deal with, respond to, or deflect chaos and confusion at the drop of a dime.
9. We must become cautious about how we respond, retaliate, or regraft our lives.
10. We must govern our motives, keeping them aligned with the Kingdom of God.
11. We must help, feed, and Bless others with no strings attached while exhibiting Spiritual Proactiveness.
12. We must do and be good, especially when bad things are happening, while examining ourselves, our fruits, our character, and the root of our issues from the inside out, not from the outside in.

But more importantly, let us align this with scripture, *"Be of the same mind toward one another. Do not set your mind on high things, but associate with the humble. Do not be wise in your own opinion. Repay no one evil for evil. Have regard for good things in the sight of all men. If it is possible, as much as depends on you, live peaceably with all men. Beloved, do not avenge yourselves, but rather give place to wrath; for it is written, 'Vengeance is Mine, I will repay,' says the Lord. Therefore 'If your enemy is hungry, feed him; If he is thirsty, give him a drink; for in so doing you will heap coals of fire on his head.' Do not be overcome by evil, but overcome evil with good."* Romans 12:16-21.

Our *Spiritual Tutor* is not designed to make us codependent; it is designed to make us interdependent, working together as a Spiritual Team in Oneness. What does this mean? We have a role to play in our *Spirit to Spirit* Relationship, and the Holy Trinity has a responsibility to us as well, similar to a parent-child relationship. All in all, regardless of who we are and why, we must come together in Earthen Vessel to complete the Heaven on Earth Experience according to the Divine Blueprint set in place. If not, we will experience a longing, thirst, hunger, void, or some form of emptiness from within, even if we are conditioned to cover it up or play possum.

In my opinion, we have been beating around the bush for too long, and it is time for us to step up to the plate and take full responsibility for our Divine Mission. What if we do not know what it is? It is time to get *In-The-Spiritual-Know*. In the same way that we can master the edifices associated with our likes or dislikes in our worldly affairs, we can also do this with our Kingdom Affairs as well. For example, if we set a goal to achieve something, we will do what it takes to get it unless someone or something stops us. Meanwhile, with our Divine Purpose, the same rules apply, but from a Spiritual Perspective, allowing our *Spiritual Tutor* to guide us or illuminate our path toward righteousness.

What does righteousness have to do with our Divine Purpose or our *Spiritual Tutor*? If we do not choose the Path of Righteousness, then we will revert to a path of unrighteousness by default, and the Holy Spirit will lie dormant when our motives are wrong, or when we are attempting to pimp God or desecrate the Blood of Jesus. As a result, we pick up a like-spirit that allows us to engage in wrongdoings, evil practices, negativity, and so on.

But here is the catch: When going to the dark side, getting the appearance of purpose, we cannot use the Blood of Jesus to cover us; we must use our own sacrifice. Unrighteousness and contempt disqualify us from using the Blood of Jesus to cover practices of ill will. As a result, we will find ourselves settling or falling under the purpose of another or outright building upon another man's foundation. Really? Yes, really! For this reason, they are called dream killers, appearing Heaven Sent, but designed to lead us straight into the Pit with a one-way ticket. Plus, this is not what the Kingdom is about. *"Therefore, do not let your good be spoken of as evil;*

for the Kingdom of God is not eating and drinking, but righteousness and peace and joy in the Holy Spirit. For he who serves Christ in these things is acceptable to God and approved by men. Therefore, let us pursue the things which make for peace and the things by which one may edify another." Romans 14:16-19.

What can we do to safeguard ourselves from the path of unrighteousness? Get on board with our *Spiritual Tutor*, regrafting ourselves into what God intended in the first place as it relates to our Divine Blueprint.

Everyone's journey is different, and we need our *Spiritual Tutor* to help us along the way. Yet, let us align this before moving on, *"Therefore, I have reason to glory in Christ Jesus in the things which pertain to God. For I will not dare to speak of any of those things which Christ has not accomplished through me, in word and deed, to make the Gentiles obedient—in mighty signs and wonders, by the power of the Spirit of God, so that from Jerusalem and round about to Illyricum I have fully preached the gospel of Christ. And so, I have made it my aim to preach the gospel, not where Christ was named, lest I should build on another man's foundation, but as it is written: 'To whom He was not announced, they shall see; And those who have not heard shall understand.' For this reason, I also have been much hindered from coming to you."* Romans 15:17-22.

Amid our uniquenesses, we are designed to exhibit the Fruits of the Spirit and Christlike Character in and around all things we do, say, and become. It gives us the ability to abound amid all things and have everything we need according to our Divine Mission, especially when we begin to live by example through the Holy Spirit. Here is a scripture we should hold dear, *"Now may the God of hope fill you with all joy and peace in believing, that you may abound in hope by the power of the Holy Spirit. Now I myself am confident concerning you, my brethren, that you also are full of goodness, filled with all knowledge, able also to admonish one another. Nevertheless, brethren, I have written more boldly to you on some points, as reminding you, because of the grace given to me by God, that I might be a minister of Jesus Christ to the Gentiles, ministering the gospel of God, that the offering of the Gentiles might be acceptable, sanctified by the Holy Spirit."* Romans 15:13-16.

What is the big deal about having a *Spiritual Tutor*, especially when we have free will to do whatever we like and whenever we want? Of course, we all have the right to live on our own terms; however, when doing so, is it fair to call on the Holy Spirit when we have not put in the time to build that relationship?

For example, this is like having a fake friend who only calls when they need something, spitting in our face as if we are a nobody, talking about us like a junk-yard dog behind our backs, and kicking dirt on us when they do not need us. Yet, when the table turns in our favor, they want to take the credit for standing by us. When, in all actuality, the truth is, they were one step away from burning the bridges on us, then a need presented itself, and they remembered us as the *ace in the hole*.

Can one imagine using the Holy Trinity as their *ace in the hole*? Although this example is sad, it is all too true. After all, this is why *"The Spirit searches all things, yes, the deep things of God."* 1 Corinthians 2:10.

Why would the Holy Spirit search within? According to scripture, *"For what man knows the things of a man except the spirit of the man which is in him? Even so no one knows the things of God except the Spirit of God."* 1 Corinthians 2:11. Bottom line, we need our *Spiritual Tutor* to search the human psyche for hidden things of the heart. We can tiptoe around, bragging about how powerful we are; however, our power is indeed limited without the Holy Spirit. How can I say such a thing, right? Well, the truth is revealed behind closed doors, with our fruits, and in our character.

In all actuality, if we are NOT aligning ourselves with Spiritual Principles, we are NOT in a Spiritual Classroom, we are doing our own thing without a conscience, and we are engaging in all sorts of debauchery. We must question whether or not the Holy Spirit is dwelling within or if it is a spirit of another kind.

What is the difference between carnality vs. Spirit Man? One is worldly, and the other is Spiritual. But let us take this a step further with 1 Corinthians 2:12-16, which says: *"Now we have received, not the spirit of the world, but the Spirit who is from God, that we might know the things that have been freely given to us by God. These things we also speak, not in words* which man's wisdom teaches but which the Holy Spirit teaches, comparing spiritual things with spiritual. But the natural man does not receive the things of the Spirit of God, for they are foolishness to him; nor can he know them, because they are spiritually discerned. But he who is spiritual judges all things, yet he himself is rightly judged by no one. For 'who has known the mind of the LORD that he may instruct Him?' But we have the mind of Christ."

To be clear, we are Spiritual Beings having a human experience. When we undercut or undermine our innate ability to make a *Spirit to Spirit* Connection back to the Source, we create a disservice for ourselves, weakening our Spiritual Bonds or Spiritual Advantage.

How do we know if we are struggling with carnality? The most prominent signs are when we have a battle with any form of envy, strife, or division, which leads to all other negative character traits, keeping us in the milking stages of our Spirituality. Is the Holy Spirit biased? Of course not. We all have the same opportunity to receive the solid foods of the Holy Spirit, but we must do our part in receiving Divine Assistance. Here is the decree associated with the 'Why' of the Holy Spirit. *"And I, brethren, could not speak to you as to Spiritual people but as to carnal, as to babes in Christ. I fed you with milk and not with solid food; for until now you were not able to receive it, and even now you are still not able; for you are still carnal. For where there are envy, strife, and divisions among you, are you not carnal and behaving like mere men?"* 1 Corinthians 3:1-3.

Regardless of where we are from, what we are doing, or how we have been conditioned, the Fruits of the Spirit and Christlike Character are needed to receive the fullness of what God has to offer. So, it behooves us to get *Spiritual Tutoring* and step into the Spiritual Classroom for the regrafting process of the Kingdom.

What makes the *Spiritual Tutoring* or *Classroom* so important? Unbeknown to most, it helps us to maximize our Seedtime and Harvest phase of living, causing all things to work in our favor. How? Once we understand and respect the fact that God is our SOURCE for all things, we can better discipline ourselves accordingly, even if the Vicissitudes of Life are pressing us to the max or we are yoked to the core. What does this mean? We are able to learn, grow, and sow back into the Kingdom without having a pity party, feeling like a victim, or seeking revenge. While at the same time, knowing if God allowed it, it is designed for our growth, benefit, and training process, all orchestrated for our good with the Spiritual Intent of Blessing us to become a Blessing.

According to the Heavenly of Heavens, the Kingdom is looking for willful usability and moldability. As it relates to the Heavenly of Heavens, here is the team-playing mindset we should develop, "*I planted, Apollos watered, but God gave the increase. So then neither he who plants is anything, nor he who waters, but God who gives the increase. Now he who plants and he who waters are one, and each one will receive his own reward according to his own labor. For we are God's fellow workers; you are God's field, you are God's building. According to the grace of God which was given to me, as a wise master builder I have laid the foundation, and another builds on it. But let each one take heed how he builds on it. For no other foundation can anyone lay than that which is laid, which is Jesus Christ.*" 1 Corinthians 3:6-11.

We must be willing to do our part in the Kingdom, ensuring our Heaven on Earth involvement is experienced inwardly and spread outwardly. However, to do so, we cannot become selfish in our attempts. "*Therefore, judge nothing before the time, until the Lord comes, who will both bring to light the hidden things of darkness and reveal the counsels of the hearts. Then each one's praise will come from God.*" 1 Corinthians 4:5.

God uses us to carry out the Mission of the Kingdom; however, we must believe in Him, ourselves, and others, extending love and hope to all regardless of our condition or the condition of another, *As It Pleases Him*. By far, this gives our *Spiritual Tutor* the common ground to mentor us according to Kingdom Standards, amid whatever or with whomever, making us a work-in-progress according to the Heavenly of Heavens.

In my opinion, life is by far the best Spiritual Classroom known to man because we learn as we go, getting hands-on experience. Although it may not feel good when we are going through it, in the end, when we win, we have first-hand knowledge, *Spirit to Spirit*, on how to position ourselves to cause things to work in our favor. More importantly, with this Spiritual Relationship, we do not have to

As It Pleases God®: Book Series

deal with the unsurety of second-hand information with zero experience, going with the flow of the *'anything goes'* way of life.

According to the Heavenly of Heavens, God will open the Curtains of Holiness on our behalf if we dare to step outside of our comfort zone to receive what He has to offer.

Chapter Four

SPIRIT TO SPIRIT

Our *Spirit to Spirit* Connection from the Heavenly of Heavens should not be taken for granted; not now, and not ever! Our Heaven on Earth Experiences are wrapped in our Level of RESPECT, *As It Pleases God.* We all want the Divine Connection, but in order to truly become Kingdomly Powerful in our *Spirit to Spirit* Connection, respectfulness is a must. If we lack respect, it is best not to pursue a *Spirit to Spirit* Connection from the Heavenly of Heavenlies until we are ready.

Unbeknown to most, defiance causes more harm to ourselves than good. If there is disrespect running through our veins, rest assured, there is unrest surrounding us. So, allow me to align this accordingly: "*Let every soul be subject to the governing authorities. For there is no authority except from God, and the authorities that exist are appointed by God. Therefore, whoever resists the authority resists the ordinance of God, and those who resist will bring judgment on themselves. For rulers are not a terror to good works, but to evil. Do you want to be unafraid of the authority? Do what is good, and you will have praise from the same.*" Romans 13:1-3.

Spirit to Spirit, here is something to think about before we go any further. Who knows our Divine Blueprint better than the Spirit of

As It Pleases God®: Book Series

God? If we lack Spiritual Respect for our Creator, will we really respect the Divine Plan? Once we get what we want from God, will we respect those beneath us or look down on them? Why do we need to know this? It is because Spirit respects Spirit, period!

As It Pleases God, if our Spiritual Senses are not up to par, recognizing the Heavenly Anointed, then we have work to do. Until we get to this point in our Spiritual Relationship, respect everyone because we will never know who He is using to test our Spirit or our Anointing.

In the Kingdom, we are a family of Oneness based upon two types of relations:

1. Spiritual Relations.
2. Human Relations.

If we miss the mark in the relational department, we will find ourselves failing at our *People Skills* and contradicting the Fruits of the Spirit, causing Reverse Relations instead. Reverse Relations are when we are doing everything against or the opposite of the Will of God, predicated on worldliness through our senses, lusts, and selfishness. For example, we are designed to love and be loved. If we are operating in hatefulness, whether within ourselves or with others, we will cause the Cycle of Life to reverse, not working in our favor because we are naturally designed to love.

Most often, amid the reversal, this is when everything falls apart, breaks, goes wrong, or we have a trail of rottenness, chaos, betrayal, debauchery, and confusion. For some, this is their norm, so they do not see a problem with this. Then, from a Spiritual Perspective, there is a problem indeed, and it is within the human psyche, spreading outwardly.

Spiritually Speaking, if we dare to turn the unrepenting Reverse Relations (*worldly to worldly*) into repenting Spiritually (*Spirit to Spirit*) with our Human (*Spirit to Man*) Relations predicated on the Fruits of the Spirit and Christlike Character, we will find that a transformation will take place from the inside out. Why would this Spiritual Transformation occur? Our Divine Blueprint is within, and we are naturally designed to exhibit Love, Joy, Peace, Patience, Kindness, Goodness, Faithfulness, Gentleness, and Self-Control. Once used, *As It Pleases God*, we will naturally activate the *Gravitational Pull* of Righteousness by default, which is already embedded in our DNA.

How will the *Gravitational Pull* of Righteousness benefit us? It makes us Spiritually Sharp and naturally friendly. Here is what Proverbs 27:17 states: "*As iron sharpens iron, so a man sharpens the countenance of his friend.*" In addition, it also bridges the gap in the transformational process, going from unrighteousness to righteousness, based upon the Spiritual Principles and Laws hidden in the Fruits of the Spirit. Really? Yes, really! Once we repent, the Spiritual Seal is called forgiveness, grace, and mercy through the Sacrificial Lamb who gave His life in ATONEMENT for us.

According to the Heavenly of Heavens, if we go against our Divine Design, the Holy Spirit must lie dormant; therefore, the human psyche takes over, doing whatever and with whomever if left ungoverned, untamed, traumatized, or uncorrected. Unbeknown to most, this indeed leads to Spiritual Blindness, Deafness, and Muteness based upon the lust of the eyes, lust of the flesh, and the pride of life. So, being that we are doing the opposite of our Blueprint, the Cycle and the Vicissitudes will serve us the opposite of righteousness on a silver platter, as we think we are right in our own eyes but all so wrong in the Eye of God and the Kingdom. How? We must account for our motives because "*Every way of a man is right in his own eyes, but the LORD weighs the hearts.*" Proverbs 21:2. The bottom line is that God is watching how we treat others when no one is looking, primarily when we do not need someone, when they appear beneath us, or when they are rough around the edges. Listen, regardless of who is trying to woo us, the question is always:

1. Are we nasty, rude, disrespectful, or unkind?
2. Are we kind, understanding, respectful, and helpful?

As It Pleases God®: Book Series

Our *People Skills* are essential in the Kingdom. If we say we represent the Kingdom and behave like a hellion on wheels, this is not godly! *"Even a child is known by his deeds, whether what he does is pure and right."* Proverbs 20:11.

Yes, we all have our moments, but our moments should be quick enough to repent and apologize amid that moment. If we train ourselves to self-correct immediately, especially when our psyche wants to show out or show its true colors, the incidents or meltdowns will decrease dramatically. How is this possible? When we align the negative fruit exhibited with the Fruits of the Spirit, or we reverse it into a positive, we can create a win-win from the inside out. Clearly, this reversal technique is not an overnight process, but when used consistently, it will regraft our lives in ways that put our enemies at bay, right before our very eyes.

What is the big deal about Relations? We all need them; however, the determining factors are in our healthy or unhealthy relations. How do we know? It varies from person to person, but if we have a problem being alone, rest assured, we are engaging in unhealthy relations. Is this not judging? Maybe or maybe not, but if there is an underlying issue preventing us from being content with ourselves and our thoughts, we have work to do.

From a Spiritual Perspective, we need time alone to hear what is going on between our ears. There are times when we block out the chatter so much that we do not realize it is drowning us in a pool of negativity, spilling over into the lives of others. So, if we do not realize or confront the fact that we are negative, we cannot regraft it into positives. Then again, if we have a hard time taking time out, we will have difficulty analyzing ourselves or doing a checkup from the neck up. As a result, it affects our *People Skills*, leading to unhealthy relations, even if we are in denial, playing pretend, or possum. But, behind closed doors, healthy or unhealthy relations are exposed without masks or the superficialities of the public eye. However, *"The first one to plead his cause seems right, until his neighbor comes and examines him."* Proverbs 18:17.

Healthy relations are based upon respect and transparency, while working together to achieve a common goal. Although the divorce rate is at 80%, it does not mean it has to remain this way. How can we change this trajectory? We must get an understanding of how to engage and disengage in and out of relationships. Listed below are a few examples of relational hypotheticals, but not limited to such:

1. If the relationship becomes competitive, where no one listens to each other, it is only a matter of time before conflict and disobedience will arise, affecting all manner of relations. *"Cease listening to instruction, my son, and you will stray from the words of knowledge."* Proverbs 19:27.

2. If we are trying to plot, attempting to change another through manipulation, or violating the will of another without working on ourselves first, this will cause a Spiritual Upset from the inside out. How? We are going to bring strife, anger, debauchery, and resentment into the relationship. *"He who plots to do evil will be called a schemer. The devising of foolishness is sin, and the scoffer is an abomination to men."* Proverbs 24:8-9.

3. If we attempt to put the outside manifestations or appearances of another above the inside man, disappointment is on the horizon. Our approach must be from the inside out, not the outside in. *"Charm is deceitful and beauty is passing, but a woman who fears the LORD, she shall be praised. Give her of the fruit of her hands, and let her own works praise her in the gates."* Proverbs 31:30-31.

4. If we are pointing fingers or bribing others without assuming responsibility, we are going to have issues. *"A gift in secret pacifies anger, and a bribe behind the back, strong wrath."* Proverbs 21:14.

5. If we complain, bicker, fuss, and fight out of envy, drawing others into our folly, we symbolically block out

righteousness due to the intents of the heart. "*Do not be envious of evil men, nor desire to be with them; for their heart devises violence, and their lips talk of troublemaking.*" Proverbs 24:1-2.

6. If we are a control freak, pouncing upon the weaknesses of another, resentfulness will soon harden the heart of the victim, who may seek revenge in due time. "*Whoever shuts his ears to the cry of the poor will also cry himself and not be heard.*" Proverbs 21:13.

7. If we abuse, misuse, or bully in the relationship, we will find the victim will withdraw Mentally, Physically, or Emotionally to protect themselves. "*A brother offended is harder to win than a strong city, and contentions are like the bars of a castle.*" Proverbs 18:19.

8. If we player hate or play mind games to exhibit or provoke jealousy, envy, or coveting, the rules of the game will eventually reverse against our favor. "*Casting lots causes contentions to cease, and keeps the mighty apart.*" Proverbs 18:18.

9. If we allow our ego to pounce upon or degrade another, we will soon bring inner shame to ourselves in the areas we are nitpicking. "*A man's stomach shall be satisfied from the fruit of his mouth; from the produce of his lips he shall be filled.*" Proverbs 18:21.

10. If we speak down or curse another, we will soon bring this folly back to ourselves. How? This negative manifestation will become unawaringly buried within our psyche. "*Death and life are in the power of the tongue, and those who love it will eat its fruit.*" Proverbs 18:21.

11. If we are consumed with lying and deception, we put all our relations at risk. "*A false witness will not go unpunished, and he who speaks lies will not escape.*" Proverbs 19:5.

12. If we do not work on or work at our relationships, they are destined to fall apart. *"A lazy man buries his hand in the bowl, and will not so much as bring it to his mouth again."* Proverbs 19:24.

In my opinion, Proverbs is the best book in the Bible to develop our *People Skills*. Frankly, this is how I developed mine. *Spirit to Spirit*, I promise it will work for anyone serious about understanding their behaviors from a Spiritual Perspective.

What are the benefits associated with the Book of Proverbs? It teaches us how to behave according to Kingdom Principles, what characteristics the Kingdom of Heaven is expecting from us, and what to nourish, cherish, pursue, or prune to keep us in an upright, standing position among the Spiritual Elites in Earthen Vessel. More importantly, according to scripture, *"The righteous man walks in his integrity; his children are blessed after him."* Proverbs 20:7. In so many words, our righteousness is not just about our benefits; it is about our Bloodline Blessings.

In pursuing a *Spirit to Spirit* Relationship with the Holy Trinity, our teachability becomes second to none. According to the Heavenly of Heavens, when we cast down worldliness and embrace the Kingdom Mentality, we become the responsibility of the Holy of Holies to train us in the ways of the Spirit. Why do we need training? To ensure we do not intertwine worldliness into Kingdom Principles, or mislead others due to our lack of understanding.

If the truth is told, most of the wolves in sheep's clothing do not realize they are behaving like a wolf or turning their prayer into a session of witchcraft. As Believers, how is it possible NOT to know the impact of our prayers? It can easily happen when operating from conditioning, cultural biases, self-induced beliefs, and passed on traditions without developing a *Spirit to Spirit* Connection.

When we do not have a full understanding of the Fruits of the Spirit, or we are not accustomed to exhibiting Christlike Character, we symbolically create what feels right to us, going through the motions. Once this happens, we cannot pinpoint the voids we feel, the trauma we cannot get over, the inner chatter that is running wild, the anger we are experiencing, the revenge we seek, and so on. As a result, this negativity spills over into our prayers without realizing what we are doing, causing us to pray amiss or have our prayers go unanswered.

Listen, my ears have been to the ground long enough to understand how the Kingdom operates, *As It Pleases God*. When someone does not fully understand Kingdom Principles and Laws, they will gravitate toward ANGRILY defending the Word of God. When in all actuality, we only need to STAND on the Word! Blasphemy, right? Wrong! The Word of God is ABSOLUTE.

When it comes down to the Holy of Holies, we must get out of our feelings, do what we have been called to do, and allow God to be God! *"And He said to me, 'Son of man, stand on your feet, and I will speak to you.' Then the Spirit entered me when He spoke to me, and set me on my feet; and I heard Him who spoke to me. And He said to me: Son of man, I am sending you to the children of Israel, to a rebellious nation that has rebelled against Me; they and their fathers have transgressed against Me to this very day. For they are impudent and stubborn children. I am sending you to them, and you shall say to them, 'Thus says the Lord GOD.'"* Ezekiel 2:1-4.

Here is a question: 'Do we see God physically fighting men?' No, we do not; everything with God is Spiritual in the Realm of the Unseen. However, He does ALLOW things to happen based upon the Systems, Cycles, and Laws already set in place, such as the Law of Gravity, Seedtime and Harvest, and so on. Now, to take this a step further, outside of what is already set in place, we will also see two things happening, especially if we DO NOT put the Holy Trinity at the forefront of our lives:

1. We will see men (mankind) fighting against each other.
2. We will see men (mankind) fighting against themselves.

If we are created in the Image of God, we must elevate ourselves to the Spiritual Realm. Frankly, this is where the battles are really taking place, causing us to feel as if it is real. When, in all actuality, we are really the culprit. What does this mean? In our world, we are reacting to life, when life is reacting to us based upon what we have set in motion with our thoughts, beliefs, actions, reactions, behaviors, and so on, giving life to our SEED producing fruit after its own kind, positively or negatively.

Why do we need to know this information? When dealing in a *Spirit to Spirit* Relationship, we cannot sit around twiddling our thumbs, ignoring our Divine Blueprint, neglecting to build ourselves up from the inside out, or reacting to people, places, and things God has already delivered us from.

Is this Biblical? Of course, here is what Jesus said to Saul, who turned Paul on the Road to Damascus, *"So I said, 'Who are You, Lord?' And He said, 'I am Jesus, whom you are persecuting.' But rise and stand on your feet; for I have appeared to you for this purpose, to make you a minister and a witness both of the things which you have seen and of the things which I will yet reveal to you. I will deliver you from the Jewish people, as well as from the Gentiles, to whom I now send you, to open their eyes, in order to turn them from darkness to light, and from the power of Satan to God, that they may receive forgiveness of sins and an inheritance among those who are sanctified by faith in Me."* Acts 26:15-18.

Well, regardless of where we are in life, our ROAD may not lead us to Damascus, but it is going to definitely lead us somewhere. However, our somewhere will determine whether our ROAD leads us into Heaven or the Pit, based upon the choices we are making on a moment-by-moment basis. For this reason, it is always best to have the Holy Spirit guiding us as we cover ourselves with the Blood of Jesus to create a Spiritual Bumper for ourselves.

What is a Spiritual Bumper? It is our BOUNCE BACK ability through grace, mercy, and forgiveness hidden in our repentance and transparency. Unbeknown to most, by owning our truth and doing the right thing, even when the wrong things are happening, it really strengthens our 'Bounce Back' or 'Give Back.'

When we are obedient in our *Spirit to Spirit* Relationship, and when we stand steadfast on God's Word in the Spirit of Righteousness, He will defend us. With this knowledge, we can contend with the wiles of the enemy while putting on the Whole Armor of God in the Realm of the Spirit.

How do we get started on our *Spirit to Spirit* Journey with the Heavenly of Heavens on our side? The first step is to make a CHOICE to do so. Secondly, willfully invite the Holy Trinity (The Father, Son, and Holy Spirit) into our lives' equation, guiding us out of darkness to the Path of Light. Thirdly, REPENT of all known and unknown atrocities hindering our walk or blocking our path toward righteousness! Why do we need to repent? Without repentance, we are symbolically telling God that we are perfect, we are not wrong about anything, all of our fruits are good, and the Spirit of Deception has clouded our sense of good judgment.

Listen, in our walk with God, we must constantly pay attention to 'What' we are doing, 'Why' we are doing it, 'Where' we are doing it, 'When' we are doing it, 'How' we are doing it, and with 'Whom.' By doing so, we are able to determine our motives of righteousness vs. unrighteousness when aligned with the Fruits of the Spirit.

Here is the Spiritual Decree set before us daily, but for some reason, the human psyche tries to forget it: *"See, I have set before you today life and good, death and evil, in that I command you today to love the LORD your God, to walk in His ways, and to keep His commandments, His statutes, and His judgments, that you may live and multiply; and the LORD your God will bless you in the land which you go to possess."* Deuteronomy 30:15-16. Some would say that was back then, and this is now. Well, the only difference from then to now is the matter of TIME, but the Spirit of God or our Divine Blueprint has not changed!

All in all, the *Ancient of Ancients* wants us to get back on track with our *Spirit to Spirit* Relationship, putting our worldliness on the back burner to possess what rightly belongs to us. Spiritually Speaking, whatever we need is already, so do not become deceived by rationalizing and justifying the Word of God, primarily when it is already written on the heart of every man, waiting for Spiritual Illumination or Redemption.

Chapter Five

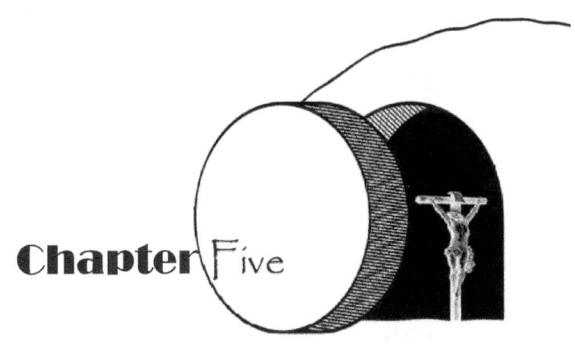

REDEEMING THE TIMES

According to the Heavenly of Heavens, in *Redeeming the Times*, the same recipe designed for elevation is the exact ingredient that can become a disaster, especially if we take God out of the equation. How do we redeem ourselves? We must become willing to purify ourselves from the inside out, from the negative characteristics causing us to become the enemy turned inward. Outside of the lack of love or the overzealous effects of having too much of it. The dynamics of hidden anger, greed, and resentment are the second most profound contributors to the issues we are facing today, breaking the broken bond of relationships from worldly to Spiritual.

Most would think we should cut off relationships with the worldly, especially when we develop a Spiritual Relationship, and this is so far from the truth. God owns it ALL! But let us align this accordingly, *"All things were made through Him, and without Him nothing was made that was made. In Him was life, and the life was the light of men. And the light shines in the darkness, and the darkness did not comprehend it. There was a man sent from God, whose name was John. This man came for a witness, to bear witness of the Light, that all through him might believe. He was not that*

Light, but was sent to bear witness of that Light. That was the true Light which gives light to every man coming into the world." John 1:3-9.*

In the Kingdom, we must learn how to deal with anyone on any level, being kind, strong, and consistently diligent with the Fruits of the Spirit and our Christlike Character. We are the Earthen Vessels used to draw people into the Light, *Redeeming the Times*. I know it can become challenging, but we must be willing to work on ourselves daily to endure the wiles of the enemy on a moment-by-moment basis. What is the purpose of doing so? The enemy will change their strategy at any given moment; therefore, we must be prepared with positive forces to rise above the under or uppercut designed to break our stride, testing our level of patience and humility.

In *Redeeming the Times*, according to the Heavenly of Heavens, we will encounter the elements of unfairness and injustice, but we do not have to engage in such behaviors. Unbeknown to most, the moment we take a stand for unselfish and wholehearted righteousness, our psyche stands at attention, waiting for instructions. Now, if we fail to feed it with the proper instructions, *As It Pleases God*, it will revert to its default mechanism, biases, conditioning, or the path of least resistance, thwarting our understanding or truth. In addition, it will also inadvertently make us appear difficult.

Our perception is subjected to worldly or deceptive measures, especially if the Word of God is not interjected into the equation or rationalization. Plus, when we do not understand others, we will naturally perceive them as problematic based on our motives.

The bottom line is that we are designed to make a difference in our ability to understand, convey, redirect, and articulate on behalf of the Kingdom to *Redeem the Times*. Now, in the process of this Spiritual Manifestation, we need the Holy Spirit and the Blood of Jesus to keep us on a straight and narrow path. If we decline in this formality, our perception can indeed get in the way of our genuine efforts, sometimes turning negatively awkward.

We have all found ourselves at some point thinking we are doing the right thing, but according to the Kingdom, *As It Pleases God*, our motives were all wrong. Or, we found ourselves feeling as if we were wrong in our charactorial approach or sight; yet, in the Kingdom, it was the right thing to do.

For instance, consider someone who is mistreated, rejected, and left to fend for themselves. As a result, this person feels foolish for showing mercy, forgiveness, and compassion, especially when those who wish to harm them ultimately fall into their own traps. They might feel annoyed, particularly when they are tempted to hold onto their anger or wish for the wrongdoers to experience their own pain. Nevertheless, their conscience prevents them from treating others as they were treated. Instead, they choose to rise above the situation, employing the Fruits of the Spirit and embodying Christlike character as their Spiritual Principles, while steering clear of any negative influences from adversaries.

When *Redeeming the Times*, we do not want to give the enemy any justifiable leverage to pounce upon or yoke us for behaving in an ungodly, negative manner, clouding our sense of reasoning and good judgment. What does this have to do with anything, especially when we feel justified? Justified or not, when we are acting and behaving foolishly, supposedly in the Name of God, it opens the door for other hypocritical behaviors, causing the Kingdom to frown upon our reckless folly.

We, as parents or guardians, attempt to save our children from the world, but we fail to train them on how to deal with, maneuver through, contend among, abound from, or create a win-win amid dire defeat. More importantly, according to scripture, we must train ourselves and our offspring to become sanctified by Divine Truths instead of worldly deception. Is this Biblical? I would have it no other way, *"But now I come to You, and these things I speak in the world, that they may have My joy fulfilled in themselves. I have given them Your word; and the world has hated them because they are not of the world, just as I am not of the world. I do not pray that You should take them out of the world, but that You should keep them from the evil one. They are not of the world, just as I am not of the world. Sanctify them by Your truth. Your word is truth. As You sent Me into the world, I also have sent them into the world. And for their sakes I sanctify Myself, that they also may be sanctified by the truth."* John 17:13-19.

In our redemptive efforts, God is a God of second, third, fourth, fifth, sixth, seventh chances, and so on. So, if we are forgiven, why are we not forgiving others? Or, better yet, why should we forgive those who have warped motives? God must judge the motives of all; however, it is our responsibility to keep the negative debris from forming by simply forgiving, moving on, and bearing no grudges. For this reason, let us deal with forgiveness first: *"Then Peter came to Him and said, 'Lord, how often shall my brother sin against me, and I forgive him? Up to seven times?' Jesus said to him, I do not say to you, up to seven times, but up to seventy times seven."* Matthew 18:21-22. Secondly, *"You shall not hate your brother in your heart. You shall surely rebuke your neighbor, and not bear sin because of him. You shall not take vengeance, nor bear any grudge against the children of your people, but you shall love your neighbor as yourself: I am the LORD."* Leviticus 19:17-18.

Truthfully, to maximize our highest and greatest potential amid *Redeeming the Times*, we must put our differences and biases away, dealing with the issues at hand in the Spirit of Righteousness, even when people spit in our face, use, mock, talk about, or disrespect us. If not, the same hang-ups we have with others, we will eventually knowingly or unknowingly yoke ourselves.

Here is what Job 17:3-9 says about this: *"Now put down a pledge for me with Yourself. Who is he who will shake hands with me? For You have hidden their heart from understanding; therefore, You will not exalt them. He who speaks flattery to his friends, even the eyes of his children will fail. But He has made me a byword of the people, and I have become one in whose face men spit. My eye has also grown dim because of sorrow, and all my members are like shadows. Upright men are astonished at this, and the innocent stirs himself up against the hypocrite. Yet the righteous will hold to his way, and he who has clean hands will be stronger and stronger."*

According to the Heavenly of Heavens, it is in our best interest to do a clean sweep of all negativity, unforgiveness, and resentment. Our Blessings are tied to overcoming the undesirable characteristics that easily beset us, and it is also associated with the intimacy we will have with God. Really? Yes, really. Here is what Psalm 24:3-5 says: *"Who may ascend into the hill of the LORD? Or who may stand in His* holy place? He who has clean hands and a pure heart, who has not lifted up his soul to an idol, nor sworn deceitfully. He shall receive Blessings from the LORD, and righteousness from the God of his salvation."

Clearly, no one is immune to negative feelings; however, our responsibility is to deal with them accordingly, ensuring they do not infect our fruits with toxins or disobediently warp our character. For this reason, it is imperative to use the Fruits of the Spirit to develop Christlike Character, warding off the provocation to further decline our Earthen Vessels, affecting our relationships and People Skills.

In *Redeeming the Times* of our past, present, and future, we do not want to position ourselves to have a temper tantrum or meltdown amid the Vicissitudes of Life. Nor do we want others to cringe when they see us coming or running for cover when we appear. For this reason, we must consistently work on ourselves to become better without having the negative characteristics of envy, jealousy, pride, coveting, anger, hatred, resentment, competitiveness, outbursts, revengefulness, or slandering to overshadow our ability to effectively communicate or cause us to run away from dealing with the inevitable.

Unfortunately, people will more than likely NOT tell us when we are repulsive. They will usually allow us to continue in our folly, hiding in the bush like a roaring lion waiting for us to trip up, then letting loose their vengeful wrath to see what we are really made of. Now, for the sake of this book, we do not want it to get to this point, so let us go a little deeper.

Regardless of who we are and why, when faced with negative character traits, emotions, behaviors, thoughts, and so on, we must eventually deal with them to avoid the cycle of déjà vu from availing ourselves, exhausting us, or our Bloodline. When aligning ourselves with the Heavenly of Heavens, we must *repent* in order to *redeem*. At the same time, most would want *Redemption* alone without getting to the root cause of the issue, trauma, condition, mindset, or whatever.

We cannot overlook the *Tilling Process*; we must lift the generational curse from the Garden of Eden to *Redeem the Times*.

As It Pleases God®: Book Series

How do we go about doing so? We must put in the work, Spiritually Tilling our own ground from the inside out and becoming our Brother's Keeper once done. If not, we will find a history of time not being on our side, including the mismanagement of it while pretending to be on top of our game. When, in all actuality, our game is on top of us with a yoke intertwined in the core of our being, disguised as something else. How so? Listed below are a few examples, but not limited to such:

- ☐ When we exclude God and are constantly missing the mark, it produces a yoke.
- ☐ When we procrastinate, delaying people, places, and things unnecessarily, it initiates a yoke.
- ☐ When we become content with unfinished projects, it indicates a yoke.
- ☐ When we have a problem multitasking and planning, it forms a yoke.
- ☐ When we remain confused about what we must do, it is due to a yoke.
- ☐ When we have a history of unhealthy or fallible relationships turning us into enemies, it is facilitated by a yoke.
- ☐ When we are always a '*Day late and a dollar short*' in life, it is a sign of a yoke.
- ☐ When we leave people worse off than when we met them, it is orchestrated by a yoke.
- ☐ When we overcommit ourselves, we become easily overwhelmed and burned out with a yoke attached.
- ☐ When we have issues communicating and are easily distracted, it reveals a yoke.
- ☐ When we are very indecisive and spend too much time on unhealthy activities, it feeds our yoke.
- ☐ When we spend too much time complicating things instead of simplifying, it ties the yoke tighter.

Yokes, or no yokes...they are real and are self-created, self-induced, and self-contained. A yoke, soul tie, or bondage contains the power we give it based on the leverage, environment, or access we provide. If we exclude God from our lives' equation, we become destined to please ourselves to our detriment, thinking we are right or justified. Moreover, if we have a desire to be redeemed, *As It Pleases God*, we must know what they are and why they are holding on for dear life within the psyche. For the record, they do not hang around for no reason; they must be fed. If we are feeding them, it is our responsibility to cease engagement with it, that, or them, and stop pretending!

The goal is to become better, making the lives of others better as well. Nevertheless, if we find ourselves on the decline from the inside out, causing a decline in the lives of others, we have work to do. To be clear, simply because we have work to do, it does not make us bad people. Remember that we all have good and bad inside of us in need of redirection; we just need to know what to do, why we are doing so, and what our triggers are.

Although most would never admit to turning into someone else that they do not recognize when triggered, nor would they admit to becoming triumphantly aggressive in their approach. But, behind closed doors, it happens all too often, mainly when we do not get what we want or our expectations are shattered. In all reality, the other person from within is really our psyche releasing itself for human display or consumption; therefore, we must be cautious, especially when we are negatively unleashing the wrath hidden in the lust of the eyes, the lust of the flesh, and the pride of life.

Why do we need to be careful about our triggers? It means self-control is not present, and our rooted trauma has not been dealt with accordingly, or *As It Pleases God*. So, if any of the three elements (the lust of the eyes, the lust of the flesh, and the pride of life) are present, we can yolk ourselves without batting an eye or giving it a second thought.

In the Kingdom, being stuck on the negative creates a great disservice to ourselves and others. It leads to some form of obstructive Mental, Physical, and Emotional violence or trauma, where we knowingly or unknowingly inflict this upon those looking up to us for answers, help, guidance, or who need what we have to offer.

As a part of *Redeeming the Times*, the Heavenly of Heavens is bringing this form of soulful lapse to our attention. If we look around, we are in a state of mass dilemma, and we cannot see that we are in such a state. Plus, it has become the norm to be disrespectful, rude, unkind, and biased with zero to no repercussions. Nevertheless, in the Kingdom, it does not go unnoticed in the Eye of God. Moreover, if He has me documenting it, *As It Pleases Him*, it is a BIG issue!

According to the Heavenly of Heavens, as we address this issue, we must know that we all have a trigger, sore spot, or something to work on, at, or through, but we do not have to lose our cool or play dirty. If we do, we can openly regain our composure, self-correct, or reverse it at that moment. We do not have to wait until we get home or in our prayer closet; we can use the Fruits of the Spirit at that very moment. If we do not know what they are, we should keep a flashcard of them in our pockets until we are well-versed in them.

So, when our psyche has a temper tantrum, attempting to embarrass or oust us, we need to put it in check by correcting it instantly, without waiting or playing clean up. By doing so, we will train ourselves to exhibit the Fruits of the Spirit and Christlike Character from the jumpstart and to think on our feet.

All in all, when making sense of our lives or when redeeming ourselves, we can better make sense of what is happening around us without allowing it to affect or get into us. How is this possible? Our Divine Blueprint is already. All we need to do is align ourselves accordingly, getting in Purpose on purpose, and the Cycle of Life will filter in or out what we need or do not need. In addition, it will also place us in a Passover Covering. In light of our faithfulness, this is when we cover ourselves with the Blood of Jesus, allowing the Holy Spirit to do what needs to be done in the delivering phase for the completion of our Divine Mission, ushering us into the *Lifestyles of the Ancient*.

Chapter Six

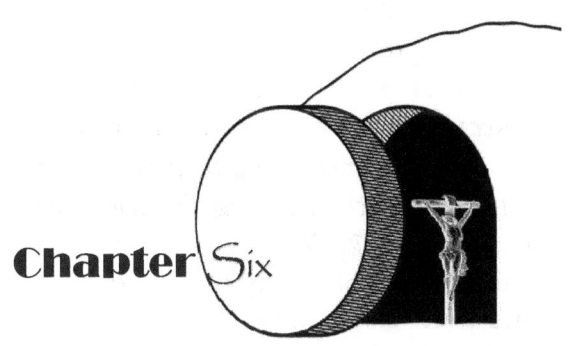

LIFESTYLES OF THE ANCIENT

Before now, the *Lifestyles of the Ancient* were not for all to understand due to certain Spiritual Seals. Nevertheless, the time has come to open the doors of Divine Wisdom for all who are willing to enter. A *Spirit to Spirit* Relationship with our Heavenly Father and Wisdom go hand-in-hand; even when He is silent, we feel unusable, we are searching for meaning, or we cannot feel His Divine Touch. Thus, it does not change the information readily available at our fingertips.

We can tiptoe around the appearance of what we perceive to be the desired *Lifestyle*. However, it looks for what we possess from within and how we handle people, places, and things outwardly when it comes down to the Kingdom, especially when no one is looking. What does this mean? We must possess the qualities and characteristics money cannot buy, contributing to our *Ancient Style of Life*, and receiving the Secrets, Mysteries, and Treasures of the Kingdom that will allow us to stay instinctually *In The Spiritual Know*.

The *Ancient of Ancients* is not playing around when it comes down to reaping Kingdom Benefits without us accounting for the cost. How does this relate to us? We want the Benefits of the Kingdom for free. Then, we sell half-truths of manipulation to others for a fee without telling them the truth about the Operative Efforts of the Kingdom, preventing them from finishing their race, *As It Pleases God*. Here is what we need to know: "*For which of you, intending to build a tower, does not sit down first and count the cost, whether he has enough to finish it—lest, after he has laid the foundation, and is not able to finish, all who see it begin to mock him, saying, this man began to build and was not able to finish.*" Luke 14:28-30.

As a Representative of the Kingdom, in our Earthen Vessels, we must work on ourselves from the inside out, bringing forth the Spiritual Truths. To be clear, God does provide handsomely for those who are in Purpose on purpose. He also makes Provision for His Vision and orchestrates a comfortable *Lifestyle* for the *Representatives of the Ancient*. However, He requires us to do our part in upholding the Fruits of the Spirit and exhibiting Christlike Character, becoming the Fountain of Wisdom for His sheep while setting an example for them to follow.

What if God does not provide for us? It may be the wrong Blueprint, our understanding of our Blueprint needs regrafting, our fruits or character are not aligning with Kingdom Expectations, or our *Spirit to Spirit* Relationship is not connecting properly amid prayer, meditating, or repenting.

Regardless of where we are on our Spiritual Journey, He does not want us to give way to the Spirit of Lack. Operating in the Spirit of Lack is not a desired Mindset of the Kingdom due to the gravitational pull associated with being disadvantaged. By far, this negative connotation of deception invokes jealousy, envy, greed, coveting, competitiveness, and so on, zapping our Divine Wisdom or sense of reasoning.

What type of Mindset should we have? The *Lifestyles of the Ancient* insist that in the regrafting phase from negative to positive, we should say this until it becomes our Bedrock of Hope: "*My God shall supply all my needs according to His riches in glory by Christ Jesus.*" Philippians 4:19.

In the Kingdom, our Spiritual Nature is not hiding from us; in all actuality, we are hiding from it. The human psyche knows it must up the ante on its attitude, behavior, and thoughts while Kingdom Proofing its efforts. What does this mean? We are held to a higher standard, and we are accountable for what we are or are not doing in or out of Kingdom Formality.

In all-knowing from the Heavenly of Heavens, WISDOM is the most prized possession known to man and the Ancient of Days. The *Lifestyles of the Ancient* want us to know that wisdom can get us stuff, but stuff cannot bring us Divine Wisdom; therefore, we are required to change our Mindset to that of the Kingdom.

Wisdom from the Ancient of Days is ready to open on our behalf, giving us the Spiritual Unction to function according to the standards set forth from the BEGINNING of time. We can pretend this information does not apply to us, only to find it does. How? Everything we need is already there! Our Blueprint is already set in motion, and the only person blocking it from coming forth is the one who does not recognize the Greatness from within.

Everyone is born a Genius; we simply forget this fact once we get a taste of worldliness in its rarest form, casting layers of debris on our Divine Wisdom to create a disconnect from the Kingdom. So much so, to the point where we think Wisdom is encapsulated in what we know, a strategy, goals, reasoning, and so on, when it is not. However, we can indeed incorporate Wisdom in them, but it is a Spiritual Standalone or Absolute, needing no help from anyone or anything; yet, it offers help to all who are justified in their efforts. What does this mean? We cannot use Divine Wisdom to conduct evil practices.

Why should we NOT use Divine Wisdom in our debaucherous efforts? It is Divine, and it is intellectually beyond our knowing capacity, training, and conditioning. The misuse of Divine Wisdom comes with a sacrificial price tag NOT covered by the Blood of Jesus. So, when attempting to misuse what is Divine or wanting a higher capacity to know things outside of their Spiritual League, one must go to the dark side to conduct this sort of folly. The moment we dare to use it in such a manner, it creates snares within the human psyche, called voids, yokes, strongholds, contention, oppression, thirsts, and fits of hunger with a BULLSEYE on our esteem and credibility.

All forms of Spiritual Disengagement are formed through the lust of the eyes, the lust of the flesh, and the pride of life. These three portals take us from a Kingdom Genius to the average worldly status. What does this mean for us? It turns our inherited Wisdom into unrecognizable sources of insecurities, weaknesses, powerlessness, and negativity while we think we are on top of the world.

Yet, the enemy is laughing in the face of those who do not know or understand who they are in the Kingdom. By failing to realize this bullseye, they fall for the okey-doke with little or no self-control, surrounded by rotten fruits and atrocious character traits! While, at the same time, yoking those who falsify their *Lifestyles as Ancient*, making them power-hungry, money-hungry, or sexually hungry.

When all is said and done, WISDOM is a GIFT that is not for sale. We will never find it packaged on a shelf, regardless of how manipulative we have become in our approach to selling it. According to the Heavenly of Heavens, this is why a lot of Spiritual Potentials or Elites get in trouble with God. How? Selling God, Divine Wisdom, Spiritual Healing, Divine Blueprints, or Kingdom Entry while NOT knowing that they are not up for the highest bidder.

Why is it a problem when Believers are able to facilitate such? Believer or not, these items are based upon our INTERNAL FACTORS, such as our charactorial traits, desires, obedience, heart posture, and discipline, *As It Pleases God*. Selling these things outside of the Divine Will of God or *As It Pleases Him* is a form of witchcraft. And, going to the dark side to obtain them, we must proceed at our own risk because the Blood of Jesus cannot be used in our folly. Really? Yes, really!

With all due respect, this is the reason why worldly individuals appear to be more prosperous than those who are Believers. How do we make this make sense? Selling or prostituting God is a big no-no! Meanwhile, unbelievers are clear about their intents; they work on their charactorial behaviors and treat people better than so-called Believers do while exercising more self-control and helping each other. As a result, God uses them based on standard principles, while the Believers are clueless about any principles, let alone Biblical Ones. Blasphemy, right? Wrong.

How is it that we know more scriptures in the Bible and do not know the Fruits of the Spirit? How is it that we do not know what God hates? Wait, wait, wait, do not answer this yet...How is it that we do not know the power of a seed?

What do we need to do to regain our Spiritual Access to Divine Wisdom? According to scripture, the *Wisdom of the Ancients* is readily available with specific conditions, but not limited to such:

1. The *Wisdom of the Ancients* will question us according to our situation, ensuring we get an understanding of our 'Why.' *"Does not wisdom cry out, and understanding lift up her voice?"* Proverbs 8:1.

2. The *Wisdom of the Ancients* requires a planned meeting place for instructions. In the beginning, this can become challenging if we are not accustomed to sitting still or taking notes. But with time, we will recognize the importance of doing so. *"She takes her stand on the top of the high hill, beside the way, where the paths meet."* Proverbs 8:2.

3. The *Wisdom of the Ancients* wants us to realize the importance of sharing Divine Wisdom with others when it is called upon. In so many words, we cannot become selfish with the Wisdom given. Wisdom is designed to Bless the receiver as they become a giver, activating the Law of Reciprocity, which keeps the Floodgates open on our behalf and that of another. *"She cries out by the gates, at the entry of the city, at the entrance of the doors: To you, O men, I call, and my voice is to the sons of men."* Proverbs 8:3-4.

4. The *Wisdom of the Ancients* wants us to become compassionate and understanding of all. Why must we be compassionate? No one is perfect, and we are all a work-in-progress, having something to work on or work at. Here is what Proverbs 8:5 states: *"O you simple ones, understand prudence, and you fools, be of an understanding heart."*

5. The *Wisdom of the Ancients* requires us to present ourselves with well-governed *People Skills*, effectively communicating in the Spirit of Excellence without allowing anything and everything to flow out of the gateway of our mouths. *"Listen, for I will speak of excellent things, and from the opening of my lips will come right things."* Proverbs 8:6.

6. The *Wisdom of the Ancients* wants us to speak the truth in the Spirit of Love, Righteousness, and Kindness. *"For my mouth will speak truth; wickedness is an abomination to my lips. All the words of my mouth are with righteousness; nothing crooked or perverse is in them."* Proverbs 8:7-8.

7. The *Wisdom of the Ancients* declares that once we understand the Systematic Processes of the Kingdom, the information needed will find us. *"They are all plain to him who understands, and right to those who find knowledge."* Proverbs 8:9.

8. The *Wisdom of the Ancients* does not want us to misuse this Spiritual Reservoir, putting worldliness or materialism above it. We should never take this invaluable commodity for granted. If our Divine Flow of Wisdom is cut off, we are left to our own devices. Personally, I would not risk it. *"Receive my instruction, and not silver, and knowledge rather than choice gold; for wisdom is better than rubies, and all the things one may desire cannot be compared with her."* Proverbs 8:10-11.

9. The *Wisdom of the Ancients* does not want us to become arrogant and prideful, engaging in all types of evil practices. *"I, wisdom, dwell with prudence, and find out knowledge and discretion. The fear of the LORD is to hate evil; pride and arrogance and the evil way and the perverse mouth I hate."* Proverbs 8:12-13.

10. The *Wisdom of the Ancients* wants us to gain Spiritual Counsel in our developmental process or Spiritual Classroom, building our strength from the inside out. *"Counsel is mine, and sound wisdom; I am understanding, I have strength."* Proverbs 8:14.

11. The *Wisdom of the Ancients* foretells that any form of Royal Priesthood is governed by the Spirit of Wisdom to judge and rule, establishing Divine Order. *"By me kings reign, And rulers decree justice. By me Princes' rule, and nobles, all the judges of the earth."* Proverbs 8:15-16.

12. The *Wisdom of the Ancients* advocates that Love and Righteousness go a lot further than what we could ever imagine, giving us the ability to call upon Divine Wisdom to assist us at the drop of a dime with Divine Provisions. *"I love those who love me, and those who seek me diligently will find me. Riches and honor are with me, enduring riches and righteousness."* Proverbs 8:17-18.

Why do we need to know about the *Wisdom of the Ancients*? It helps us perfect the Fruits of the Spirit and our Christlike Character, putting the finishing touches on our level of impact in the Kingdom and Divine Blessings. Here is what the Bible says, *"My fruit is better than gold, yes, than fine gold, and my revenue than choice silver. I traverse the way of righteousness, in the midst of the paths of justice, that I may cause those who love me to inherit wealth, that I may fill their treasuries."* Proverbs 8:19-21.

As It Pleases God®: Book Series

In the Kingdom, we deal with two types of *Lifestyles*: The '*For Show*' and the '*For Sure*.' When we are moved to put on a *Show* to impress, persuade, or show status, we have God all wrong. He is looking for those who are *Sure* about their Blessings, Favor, Provision, or Blueprint, possessing the courage to move forward in His Will and Ways without distractions from those who are hung up on material gain.

If one has not noticed by now, those who are money-hungry or lovers of money will sell their souls at the drop of a dime. According to the Heavenly of Heavens, they are the most conniving, scheming, using, and unfaithful individuals known to man due to their inherent yoking factors related to the lust of the eyes, the lust of the flesh, and the pride of life.

In addition, without pointing the finger, they also possess character flaws, driving a wedge in the heart of the righteous, hanging the innocent out to dry without offering a helping hand, or kicking people when they are down for a feeling of superiority or control. All in all, it is reflected in their fruits and character traits by default, regardless of the type of mask they assume.

Hence, the *Ancient of the Ancients* is interjecting Divine Wisdom into our *Lifestyles* to save the human psyche from self-destructing, giving us hope and another chance to get whatever it is right. How do we recognize this type of individual? Listed below are a few recognizable factors, but not limited to such:

1. We must pay attention to their *Fruits*. Beyond a shadow of a doubt, our fruits have a way of ratting us out without us realizing what it is doing until it is done. What is the purpose of this? Unbeknown to most, there is a big difference in attempting to clean up, prune, or do something about our fruits as opposed to allowing them to remain As-Is, denied, downplayed, or outright hidden.

2. We must pay attention to negative or condescending actions, beliefs, behaviors, desires, words, or responses. Besides, from much experience, these are usually the ones

who forget where God brought or delivered them from. So, if we ask the right fact-finding questions, we can narrow down the root of their fruit without clueing them in on what we are doing or becoming fooled by their *Lifestyle*.

3. We must pay attention to their *People Skills*. Communication is everything; if we fail to communicate effectively, our relationships fall apart by default, be it public, private, exclusive, or workable relations. To be clear, we do not have to agree on all things to be amicable, kind, humble, and patient. Even if people rub us the wrong way, we still do not have to 'Show Out' or 'Put on a Show,' especially when we have the Fruits of the Spirit and Christlike Character at our beck and call. We cannot go wrong with Kingdom Mannerability.

4. We must pay attention to their *Level of Respect*. Listen, if someone does not respect their elders, authorities, rules, or laws, beware. For example, if a person is trying to woo me and does not respect their parents, I back up, period!

Frankly, I do not care how much money, status, or fame they have—disrespectfulness is not for me. Is this not judging someone? No, it is called paying attention, becoming astutely aware of the generational curses following a person who does not honor their mother or father. Really? Yes, really!

Listen, if disrespectfulness is taking place, and repentance is not established or occurs, the curse is set in motion. It cannot be reversed until the person who set it in motion repents and regrafts the root of this behavior. For me, I do not play around with curses of such magnitude. Unbeknown to most, this is a Bloodline Curse, and if a person does not see a problem with their behavior, then self-control is not in place, rotten fruits are already set in motion, disobedience is on the horizon, and history will repeat itself.

More importantly, this does not happen from the outside in, but from the inside out, plaguing the human psyche.

5. We must take into account the *Level of Tolerance*. If they have little or no tolerance for people, places, and things, this should be a RED FLAG for us. If we violate our conscience, we bring the intolerance to our level of being with a gravitational pull from their psyche to ours. What does this mean? For example, if they are battling with the Spirit of Anger, then we will inherit it if we bond with it through the lust of the eyes, the lust of the flesh, or the pride of life. What does the pride of life have to do with anything? It is usually through our pride that we do not let go of those who vex our Spirit.

6. We must pay attention to their *Level of Humility*. In the Kingdom, pompousness is a recipe for disaster. It brings about the Rod of Correction faster than disobedience. How is this possible? Disobedience should be corrected before pompousness, right? In worldly means, this would be the case, but when dealing with Kingdom Principles, we deal with the ROOT.

In order for disobedience to take place, most often, it is due to the root of pompousness; therefore, the Bible frowns upon this characteristic. This underlying characteristic leads to all forms of evil. For this one, let us align it with James 4:16-17: *"But now you boast in your arrogance. All such boasting is evil. Therefore, to him who knows to do good and does not do it, to him it is sin."*

Furthermore, when someone lacks humility, they tend to lose control of their tongue as well, saying things that should not be uttered. What do we need to do? Repent of this behavior, and become humble; but more importantly, here is what the scriptures tell us, *"The fear of the LORD is to hate evil; pride and arrogance and the evil way and the perverse mouth I hate."* Proverbs 8:13.

7. We must pay attention to their *Lovability*. The *Wisdom of the Ancients* warns us about those who are heartless, conscienceless, and victimizing. If we encounter someone hateful, cruel, evil, biased, vindictive, prideful, jealous, envious, competitive, or covetous, we must exercise extreme caution around them.

   To be clear, it does not mean they are a bad person; however, it is only a matter of time before we become a victim. If we are not strong enough to handle the trauma, it is best to treat them with a long-handled spoon. When we are able to love God, ourselves, and others with no strings attached, treating everyone with outright dignity, we are well on our way to doing great work from the inside out.

8. We must pay attention to their *Consistency*. Those who are all over the place Mentally, Physically, Emotionally, and Spiritually indicate unsurety regarding their Gifts, Calling, Talents, Purpose, or Creativity. By far, these are the ones who have sticky fingers of inconsistency, taking, touching, or manipulating what does not belong to them. Better yet, this form of insecurity can become our kryptonite, especially when left uncorrected, unresolved, unrepentant, or unaddressed.

9. We must pay attention to how well they own their *Truth*. If we encounter someone who does not assume responsibility or always makes excuses, beware. Passing the buck is an automatic sign of recklessness, irresponsibility, or wallowing in untruthfulness. Also, it is symbolically telling the Heavenly of Heavens that we are complete, or we do not have anything to work on or work at. The *Wisdom of the Ancients* wants us to know that our internal security begins with being true to ourselves, owning our truth, or repenting of the lies we keep telling ourselves, while becoming a work-in-progress.

10. We must pay attention to their *Level of Authenticity*. Faithfulness and trustworthiness go a long way in the Kingdom. If God can trust us, there is no limit on what we can achieve or what He will do for us. However, if we cannot trust a person as far as we can see them, then it is best to save ourselves from heartache. Unrest within the human psyche is traumatizing for anyone dead set on deception; it will lead both into a ditch, similar to the blind leading the blind.

11. We must pay attention to their *Helpfulness*. Suppose a person can sit back, avoid, or watch a person suffer without lending a helping hand. If it is within their power to do so, something is definitely wrong with their genetic makeup. Selfishness is not of God, period.

12. We must pay attention to their *Words*. What comes out of our mouths tells the world who we are, as well as the contents of our hearts. Therefore, we should set a guard over our mouths, giving thought to every word. They are a direct reflection of who we are, not who we pretend to be; we can only put on a show for so long before our words ensnare us without us knowing.

Once again, keep in mind that we are all different, so we cannot limit ourselves or others; however, we must master the ability to relate to anyone, on any level, and from any background. We will never know WHO or WHAT God is using; therefore, if we fail the test, rejecting *What* or *Who* He sent to BLESS us, we may have to hang our heads down in shame because we missed the Spiritual Marking or Cue. How? It is often due to some form of Spiritual Blindness, Deafness, or Muteness, predicated upon some form of lust of the eyes, lust of the flesh, or pride of life, dividing us from the inside out. Frankly, this all happens without us realizing what is taking place until the Divine Unveiling. We will appear right in our own eyes and all too wrong in the Eye of God.

Listen, and listen to me well. With all due respect, we are a diversified people. If we choose to become divided Mentally, Physically, Emotionally, and Spiritually due to a Superficial Lifestyle of worldliness, it will be to our detriment, crushing us to the core in due time. Why would this crush us? Suppose we portray ourselves as a Spiritual Elite, rejecting the Earthen Vessel that God sent due to some form of bias. In this case, we set ourselves up to become symbolically broken until we return to Him in a repentant state of being.

The *Lifestyles of the Ancient* are designed to BLESS us to become a Blessing. As a Word to the Wise, God will never send what we need packaged the way we envision. Nor will He present it idolistically the way the world would package it.

What is the purpose of God tricking us? He is not tricking us; we trick ourselves based on our thwarted perception of self-gratification without using our Spiritual Intuition or Discernment, *As It Pleases Him*. If we were in a Spiritual Relationship as we ought, the Holy Spirit would have informed us prior to whatever or whomever. So, if we DO NOT get the message from the Heavenly of Heavens, we may miss out, reject, or neglect whatever or whomever. As a result, we cannot lay the blame elsewhere.

Why can't we blame God for NOT informing us about something or someone? First, we should have taken the opportunity to examine the Spiritual Fruits as our secret ONE-UP from the Heavenly of Heavens. Secondly, having a *Spirit to Spirit* Connection would have advised us of the Corner Stone or Stepping Stone we are dealing with, especially when embarking upon the *Lifestyles of the Ancient*. Is this Biblical? Of course, "*Jesus said to them, 'Have you never read in the Scriptures: The stone which the builders rejected has become the Chief Cornerstone. This was the LORD's doing, and it is marvelous in our eyes?' Therefore, I say to you, the Kingdom of God will be taken from you and given to a nation bearing the fruits of it. And whoever falls on this stone will be broken; but on whomever it falls, it will grind him to powder.*" Matthew 21:42-44.

As It Pleases God®: Book Series

Why do we need the *Spirit to Spirit* Connection when dealing with the *Lifestyles of the Ancient* or our *Cornerstone*? It helps keep us aligned with our Divine Blueprint, ensuring we do not miss our Spiritual Cue or become a footstool, even if we have a few mishaps along the way. The moment we begin to pride ourselves on unrepentant or uncorrected worldliness or willful debauchery, we become divided from the Kingdom, regardless of how well we pretend.

Unbeknown to most, inner division is much more invasive than outer division. How is this possible? The hidden impact of what we cannot see packs a more powerful punch than what we can see coming. Truthfully, we cannot prepare for the unseen, especially when our Spirit is asleep, and we are Spiritually Blind, Deaf, Mute, Dull, or Stiff-Necked.

As a result of battling the unseen, we end up fighting against ourselves, not knowing what we are really fighting for unless we involve the Holy Trinity. Here is what we must know: *"So, He called them to Himself and said to them in parables: 'How can Satan cast out Satan?' If a kingdom is divided against itself, that kingdom cannot stand. And if a house is divided against itself, that house cannot stand. And if Satan has risen up against himself, and is divided, he cannot stand, but has an end. No one can enter a strong man's house and plunder his goods, unless he first binds the strong man. And then he will plunder his house."* Mark 3:23-27.

How do we prevent ourselves from becoming a victim? Here is what the *Ancient of Ancients* wants us to know, but not limited to such:

1. We must pride ourselves on making good, sound decisions without exhibiting recklessness, making excuses, or engaging in defiant debauchery.

2. We must make our best attempts not to judge because we do not know what Spirit is behind whatever or whomever. Still, we must understand or recognize the FRUITS of another or character traits having the potential to affect us or our Bloodline. Meanwhile, exhibiting the Fruits of the Spirit and Christlike Character to deflect negativity. Is this

not judging? When we redirect the Spiritual Checklist toward ourselves, it is not judging; it is called Spiritual Awareness, especially when we must pinpoint the areas in which we need to set an example or proactively offer help. If we do not know what we are dealing with, then we do not know what to do, what to counteract, or why.

On the other hand, if we are pointing the finger, attempting to degrade, demean, or dismantle, assassinating the character or fruits of another, while making fun of them or talking about them in a negative demeanor, then this is judging.

3. We must respect another person's opinion or faith. Everyone has a right to believe whatever they like as a part of our free will; however, it is our responsibility to set an example for them by using our *People Skills*. We all have our own Spiritual Journey, and no one is 100% right or wrong. There is always an element of truth; it is only a matter of right vs. wrong, good vs. bad, positive vs. negative, just vs. unjust, Kingdom vs. worldly, and so on. In Spiritual Duality, even if we disagree, we should never mistreat someone or show an unkind face in the Name of God. For the record, it is not the Spirit of God behaving in such a manner! From experience, He will take the least likely and make them likely in our face!

4. We must get rid of our hidden or open biases and conditioning. Why must we rid ourselves of them? Our personal perspectives may not be God's Perspective, *As It Pleases Him*. Therefore, we must align ourselves with the Word of God, ensuring we understand what He is expecting from us.

5. We must become selfless in the Eye of God. He frowns upon selfishness because it makes us self-centered, wanting to keep everything for ourselves while breaking the Spiritual

Flow. For example, if God is feeding us Divine Wisdom, and it stops at us or we use it to manipulate, then Divine Wisdom will break us or our flow by default. As a result, we become UNUSABLE in the Kingdom.

6. We must become transparent, owning our truth. Hidden matters of deception keep the human psyche from healing as it should. Instead, we contribute to the walls erected to block our inner selves, developing all sorts of masks. Whereas, the moment we open ourselves up to our truth, we are better able to heal within the imperials of our freedom.

7. We must be willing to become an expert in our Gifts, Calling, Talents, Purpose, or Creativity, working on them daily with one day of rest. Why do we need to rest? According to the Heavenly of Heavens, it gives God, our Gifts, Calling, Talents, Purpose, or Creativity rest, respect, and rejuvenation.

In addition, it helps us to understand our Blueprint a little better, keeping us from running around trying to do everything that does NOT fit into the Divine Plan, *As It Pleases God*.

What if we feel the urge to do something on the one day of rest? There are times when we will get a Spiritual Urge on this one day. There is no need for alarm, especially when obedience is required of us from our Heavenly Father. All it means is that God is saving someone's life or someone needs what we have to offer due to its time sensitivity. For this reason, we need to have the *Spirit to Spirit* Connection, understanding when to stand up or stand down when called upon by the Heavenly of Heavens. Just as we have respect for God, He has respect for us as well; therefore, this will not be a continuous process.

Rest, respect, and rejuvenation are prerequisites of the Kingdom, giving us time to build relations with our family and solidify our foundation. From a Divine Perspective, to keep our homes from falling apart, we need at least one day of family bonding without worldly distractions. This one day is not set in stone as long as it is done and everyone understands the meaning of Restful Bonding.

8. We must become steadfast in righteousness while not being moved by negativity or succumbing to breaking under pressure. We must be able to think positively on our feet while exhibiting the Fruits of the Spirit and Christlike Character without deviation.

9. We must pride ourselves in taming the lust of the eyes, the lust of the flesh, and the pride of life, ensuring they do not become our impending kryptonite amid our peak performance. It causes us to play ourselves short or block our own Blessings. When we are at our best, our hidden or open habits linking to these three portals open the door to sifting, yoking, or oppression.

    In order to genuinely become the best of the best in or out of the Kingdom, we must close the door on these negative portals. By doing so, it levels the playing field. What if it does not? Listen, the *'Cream of the Crop'* will always rise to the top in due season, especially if they continue to work on themselves, Spiritually Tilling their own ground, stepping up their game positively, and putting the Will of God at the forefront, *As It Pleases Him*.

10. We cannot ignore or talk down to Divine Wisdom. According to the *Ancient of Ancients*, we do not want to reject Wisdom. It has a way of speaking to us, guiding us in the right direction, or becoming deafly silent, allowing us to give way to our own folly, dire consequences, and constant defeat.

11. We must develop a private and intimate relationship with the Holy Trinity, becoming rooted and grounded in the

Word of God. We do not want to become swayed by worldliness, causing us to second-guess God, the power or guidance of the Holy Spirit, and the Blood of Jesus. Plus, we need to be able to call upon Spiritual Backup at the drop of a dime, knowing beyond a shadow of a doubt that Divine Intervention will show up on our behalf in full Spiritual Armor.

12. We must willfully use the Fruits of the Spirit and Christlike Character to become better daily without settling for defeat. When gaining our Spiritual Keys to the Kingdom of Heaven, it chooses who gains Spiritual Access and who will not, based on our heart and mind postures.

The *Lifestyles of the Ancient* says we can tiptoe around these Spiritual Principles, as well as the inner chatter surrounding us or taking place from within. Yet, when it comes down to the Kingdom, the negativity from within must be corrected to positivity, creating a win-win out of everything. If not, with all due respect, we will become an undercover hypocritical shyster, appearing right in our own eyes.

How can I say such a thing, right? If I do not tell the truth, then who will? I will not sit back and allow us to humiliate ourselves in the Name of God while behaving with such putridness, misrepresenting the Kingdom of Heaven. If we do not believe this to be true, all we need to do is check our thoughts, actions, beliefs, feelings, reactions, and most of all, what we are secretly saying to ourselves, especially when we do not get what we want, we are betrayed, or someone offends us. We will find out whether or not Divine Wisdom can reside, ushering us into Greatness or the abyss.

According to the Heavenly of Heavens, everyone desires a 'Better Lifestyle,' even if we cannot see our better amid living our best life due to selfishness, conditioning, ungratefulness, biases, jealousy, envy, coveting, or competitiveness. How can we make this make sense? If we are born into a particular environment, it is all we know until we learn something different or get a complete understanding of our lifestyle.

For example, if a child is born into poverty, they will never know they are poor if they do not surround themselves with children who are NOT impoverished. When they are exposed to another environment that appears better than what they are accustomed to, they will begin to experience negative feelings, emotions, and thoughts. If they are NOT taught otherwise or do not understand their 'Why' in life, these feelings will fester negatively due to the illusion of deprivation.

On the other hand, if we have a child of privilege, most often, they do not understand how to deal with lack, and they feel as if they should have the desires of their heart, whether good, bad, or indifferent. I understand we all want the best for ourselves and our children; however, according to the Kingdom, we must choose a straight, narrow, and positive path for all. Why must we choose in such a manner? We have those who are conditioning themselves and their children that they are better than others, as opposed to learning how to RELATE to those who are different or less fortunate, how to become GRATEFUL in all things, and how to develop confidence from the inside out, not from the outside in.

As a result of being taught privileged pompousness or the lack of self-control as a child, if they do not get what they want and when, they experience the same negative attributes of an impoverished child, inadvertently putting them in the same category without realizing the implications of doing so. Now, according to the Heavenly of Heavens, due to the lack of understanding, they learn how to cover negative attributes up by bragging, bullying, temper tantrums, and manipulating those who appear underprivileged unless they are taught otherwise.

All in all, positive or negative characteristics begin in our childhood, snowballing throughout time, intensifying or justifying traumas, thirsts, or pangs of hunger. If negativity is left uncorrected with truth and positivity, it overlaps into adulthood, embedding negative roots into our psyche so deep, it will take the Holy Trinity to help us uproot and regraft the negative to positive with the Fruits of the Spirit.

As it relates to the *Lifestyles of the Ancient*, the main difference in all things, be it worldly or Spiritual, and our true level of Status in or out of the Kingdom is *Self-Control*. It leads us, our children, or our Bloodline into our Heaven on Earth Experience or the Abyss with a one-way ticket. We can blame it on everything else in life or make excuses, but when it comes down to the human psyche, the *Control of Self* bridges the gap to the three portals ensnaring all mankind: the lust of the eye, the lust of the flesh, and the pride of life.

In perfecting our routines, habits, or regimes, we must govern ourselves accordingly, *As It Pleases God* to get to the ROOT of our control or the lack of it to partake of the *Grandfather Clause*. It is our God-Given right to have and become the best of the best, *As It Pleases Him*. Then again, if we do not want to do what it takes to get it, we also have the free will right to pass the Spiritual Mantle to the next person or settle for mediocrity. However, if we forfeit it, we have no reason to complain to God about anything or anyone, especially when He has given us the Spiritual Information, Tools, and Principles on a SILVER PLATTER.

Chapter Seven
GRANDFATHER CLAUSE

Our Forefathers have gone to battle for us in ways we would never be able to comprehend because we are indeed living the Blessings from their sweat and blood. Yet, we have the nerve to become ungrateful for the good life in which we live. What is more, we pick on or bully those who appear to have less than us based on our biases, perceptions, or conditioning, especially when inner wealth is more valuable than anything known to man.

Unbeknown to most, when there is something that money cannot buy, it creates exceptional VALUE for the Mind, Body, Soul, and Spirit. Our Forefathers knew about this, but what happened to us? We have become trapped by the ways of man, overlooking the Will of God, *As It Pleases Him*, only to please ourselves. For this reason, this chapter is designed to bring us into Spiritual Alignment with the *Grandfather Clause*, designed to help us recognize our Blessings in a whole new LIGHT.

Who knows the Mind of God, right? Wrong! It is written all over the Bible, hidden in plain sight. Yet, we miss it all the time. So, for the sake of the Ancient of Ancients, our Forefathers have a *Grandfather Clause* set in motion among the Realm of the Spirit on our behalf. How is this possible when we are in the NOW, and that was back then? Unfortunately, we are trapped in time, but the Mission of God must be fulfilled based upon a *Spirit to Spirit Connection*, not a man-to-man judicial system. What does this mean? We do not determine who makes it to Heaven, nor can we condemn someone to the abyss.

Regardless of how we point the finger, the number of curses we loom, or how many rocks we throw, we have all fallen short in the Eye of God and needed some form of forgiveness, mercy, or grace. Plus, we all have something to deal with; therefore, we should not judge the story of another man, or we will bring that same Spirit back to our house, especially without having all the facts. Blasphemy, right? Wrong. *"Judge not, that you be not judged. For with what judgment you judge, you will be judged; and with the measure you use, it will be measured back to you."* Matthew 7:1-2.

To be clear, we are NOT speaking of our Judicial System governing the Laws of the Land; we are dealing with a Spiritual System governing mankind, *As It Pleases God*.

We are here to complete our Divine Mission, not judging or degrading another based on our conditioning, biases, and perceptions. God loves us all, and He is the Creator of it all, and we cannot determine what He is doing in the life of another without the utterance of the Holy Spirit. Therefore, we should not judge, circumvent the Will of God, or place ourselves above Him. For this reason, He requires outright love, humility, and respect.

On the other hand, we are required to examine our fruits or charactorial traits and those of another to judge ourselves, perfect the Fruits of the Spirit, exhibit Christlike Character, or get an understanding of what or who we are dealing with. Yet, we must know the difference to avoid bringing condemnation back to our house.

How do we know the difference? The moment we begin to negatively point the finger, criticize, degrade, blame, or turn up our noses without the correction of the Holy Spirit, this is an indication of Spiritual Contempt. Here is a scripture, *"Therefore whoever eats this bread or drinks this cup of the Lord in an unworthy manner will be guilty of the body and blood of the Lord. But let a man examine himself, and so let him eat of* the bread and drink of the cup. For he who eats and drinks in an unworthy manner eats and drinks judgment to himself, not discerning the Lord's body. For this reason, many are weak and sick among you, and many sleep. For if we would judge ourselves, we would not be judged. But when we are judged, we are chastened by the Lord, that we may not be condemned with the world." 1 Corinthians 11:27-32.

All in all, Jesus is the Spiritual Atonement for our sins, ensuring we do not have to make any more bloody sacrifices. If, for some reason, we are making them, it is not for the God Almighty of the Heavenly of Heavens!

The Holy Spirit is our Spiritual Guide and Teacher, leading us to the Light or placing us into a Spiritual Classroom. Amid all, we are used in Earthen Vessel in cultivating or facilitating such tasks, but we are not the enforcers of the Divine Covenant. How is this possible? The Spiritual Covenant is written within each person, and they are accountable for their own due diligence.

How can we make this make sense, especially when we cannot see our hearts to read what the Divine Covenant is? We need a *Spirit to Spirit* Connection, *As It Pleases God* to unveil the veiled. Please allow me to Spiritually Align: *"For this is the covenant that I will make with the house of Israel after those days, says the LORD: I will put My laws in their mind and write them on their hearts; and I will be their God, and they shall be My people. None of them shall teach his neighbor, and none his brother, saying, 'Know the LORD,' for all shall know Me, from the least of them to the greatest of them. For I will be merciful to their unrighteousness, and their sins and their lawless deeds I will remember no more. In that He says, 'A new covenant,' He has made the first obsolete. Now what is becoming obsolete and growing old is ready to vanish away."* Hebrews 8:10-13.

How can we capitalize on the *Grandfather Clause*? Strategically and *As It Pleases God*! If the goal is to please ourselves, in due time, we will 'get got' by the wiles of the enemy. We cannot violate Spiritual Laws or Covenants. What if we do not know them? Then it behooves us to stick to using the Fruits of the Spirit and exhibiting Christlike Character; they provide a Spiritual Safety Net for us.

As It Pleases God®: Book Series

If we pride ourselves on living fancy-free, creating all types of atrocities in the Eye of God due to ignorance or the lack of understanding, we will become easy BAIT without knowing it. Now, what the BAIT is or is not becomes based on our weakest, denied, or traumatized link, so it will not be the same for everyone. What is the purpose of becoming BAIT for the enemy? The enemy is trying to get us to void the *Grandfather Clause* over our lives because the enemy lacks the authority to cancel what is DIVINE. Nonetheless, if we do it to ourselves or know nothing about it, then who gets the last laugh?

What about the *Grandmother Clause*? To be clear, before we move on, we have had some fantastic grandmothers; however, the *Grandfather Clause* incorporates both because they are ONE with the Holy of Holies. What does this mean? In the Kingdom, they are not divided. Listen, solid foundations are built and molded in Oneness with Divine Order set in place. Here is what Matthew 12:25 says, *"Every Kingdom divided against itself is brought to desolation, and every city or house divided against itself will not stand."*

Do we not have free will to disagree? Of course, we do; however, it does not mean we must become divided in doing so. We must have respect for the opinions and differences of others without getting out of character, while assuming responsibility to do the right thing regardless. How can we strategically maximize the *Grandfather Clause* to help us with lifelong skills? Listed below are a few ways, but not limited to such:

1. As *Leaders*, we must have a desire to maximize our highest and greatest potential toward righteousness.
2. As *Leaders*, we must present ourselves appropriately in public and private arenas.
3. As *Leaders*, we must be faithful to our partners.
4. As *Leaders*, we must become pleasant to be around.
5. As *Leaders*, we must be willing to help, share, and teach others.

6. As *Leaders*, we must avoid becoming drunkards, losing our sense of good judgment of sobriety.
7. As *Leaders*, we must avoid becoming violent, abusive, or abrasive.
8. As *Leaders*, we must not become greedy, lustful, or reckless.
9. As *Leaders*, we must not become quarrelsome, chaotic, controversial, or instigators.
10. As *Leaders*, we must avoid becoming covetous, competitive, or manipulative.
11. As *Leaders*, we must avoid becoming unruly, ungoverned, or indecisive.
12. As *Leaders*, we must avoid becoming rebellious and prideful.

We can use this as a checklist, or we can use 1 Timothy 3:1-6 as a reference: *"This is a faithful saying: If a man desires the position of a bishop, he desires a good work. A bishop then must be blameless, the husband of one wife, temperate, soberminded, of good behavior, hospitable, able to teach, not given to wine, not violent, not greedy for money, but gentle, not quarrelsome, not covetous. One who rules his own house well, having his children in submission with all reverence (for if a man does not know how to rule his own house, how will he take care of the church of God?); not a novice, lest being puffed up with pride he fall into the same condemnation as the devil."*

As we move on, in an information-driven society, when we preface the mother or father with the word *Grand*, it is intended to take an ordinary mother and father to the next level of outstanding, while propelling their Bloodline into *Greatness* on another level in the Spirit of Excellence. How is this possible? With a Spiritual Grandeur approach to our Bloodline, we determine the lifeline by building, pruning, sowing, tilling, and growing it with the Spiritual Principles of Wisdom, *As It Pleases God*.

Furthermore, if we desire to LEAD our Bloodline with the *Grandfather Clause* in hand, we cannot go wrong in the Will of God, using the Fruits of the Spirit and exhibiting Christlike Character. In the Kingdom, the *Grandfather Clause* is predicated on our *Spirit to*

Spirit Relations and *People Skills*. If we perfect those, becoming a work-in-progress, our Divine Blueprint will be fulfilled, paving the way to the Kingdom from *generation to generation*.

Now, if we dare to get out of the system of worldliness and into God's Head, He will restructure our Mindset into a Heavenly Stratosphere, putting our enemies to boot. What does this mean? Our Creative Genius can come forth, strategizing in ways that our enemies can never articulate, period. However, they can emulate, but cannot outdo the Creator of it all. He is always a step ahead, step above, and step beyond whatever is designed to distort our Divine Blueprint; thus, we need to know this beyond a shadow of a doubt. If not, we open ourselves up to deception, distortion, dismantling, or disenfranchising. How do we avoid this? Listed below are a few ways, but not limited to such:

1. Trust God for *'Safety.'* *"Preserve me, O God, for in You I put my trust."* Psalm 16:1.

2. Train the human psyche to *'Understand'* that everything *'Good'* comes from Above. *"O my soul, you have said to the LORD, 'You are my Lord, my goodness is nothing apart from You.'"* Psalm 16:2.

3. We must be *'In the Spiritual Know'* about being Spiritually Chosen by God for a specific PURPOSE while doing everything in the Spirit of Excellence. *"As for the saints who are on the earth, "They are the excellent ones, in whom is all my delight."* Psalm 16:3.

4. We must *'Cast Down'* idolatry while avoiding putting anything or anyone above the Holy Trinity or the Kingdom of God. *"Their sorrows shall be multiplied who hasten after another god; their drink offerings of blood I will not offer, nor take up their names on my lips."* Psalm 16:4.

5. We must *'Involve'* God in our Divine Blueprint, *As It Pleases Him*, because only He has all the unadulterated and unbiased instructions. *"O LORD, You are the portion of my inheritance and my cup; You maintain my lot."* Psalm 16:5.

6. We must *'Heed'* to the Divine Instructions given in our *Spirit to Spirit* Relationship, as well as when He drops the information right in our laps, guiding us in the right direction to take possession of our Birthrights. *"The lines have fallen to me in pleasant places; yes, I have a good inheritance."* Psalm 16:6.

7. We must *'Exalt'* God and the Heavenly of Heavens. It is a formal *'Give-Back'* for Divine Counsel from the Holy Spirit and the Covering of the Blood of Jesus. With this sort of reverence, it will guide us to the Light in our moments of darkness, especially when the Vicissitudes of Life put us in a Spiritual Classroom or when it puts us to the test to see what we are made of. *"I will bless the LORD who has given me counsel; my heart also instructs me in the night seasons."* Psalm 16:7.

8. We must *'Place'* God first before all things; it helps clear our Spiritual Eyes, Ears, and Mouth, allowing us to see people, places, and things from His point of view. *"I have set the LORD always before me; because He is at my right hand I shall not be moved."* Psalm 16:8.

9. We must *'Exhibit'* authentic happiness and joy in all things, regardless of how it may appear to the naked eye. God hides a win-win in everything! We simply must *know* it exists, *find* it, *understand* its purpose, and *share* our findings as a Spiritual Seed, sowing back into the Kingdom without becoming restless and hopeless in doing so. *"Therefore, my*

heart is glad, and my glory rejoices; my flesh also will rest in hope." Psalm 16:9.

10. We must 'Know' God will deliver us, especially if we use the Fruits of the Spirit and Christlike Character as our Weapon of Warfare. "For You will not leave my soul in Sheol, nor will You allow Your Holy One to see corruption." Psalm 16:10.

11. We must 'Ask' and 'Trust' God for Divine Direction, Information, or Revelation, leading the way of our Spiritual Path for our Heaven on Earth Experience. "You will show me the path of life." Psalm 16:11a.

12. We must 'Focus' on the *Fullness* of the Kingdom, without falling prey to the emptiness or negativity of the worldly system in which we live. If we stay on the positive side of the spectrum, we give ourselves a fighting chance from the inside out. "*In Your presence is fullness of joy; at Your right hand are pleasures forevermore.*" Psalm 16:11b.

What can we do to cause the *Grandfather Clause* to work on our behalf, especially when we are new at this? We must become Spiritually Aware while Spiritually Aligning ourselves accordingly. According to what? Everyone is different; therefore, our accordingly must be ushered in by the Holy Spirit with the sacrificial Blood of Jesus, covering us from head to toe, inside and out, and roundabout the way.

What is the big deal about our Forefathers? According to 2 Timothy 1:3-6, it says, "*I thank God, whom I serve with a pure conscience, as my forefathers did, as without ceasing I remember you in my prayers night and day, greatly desiring to see you, being mindful of your tears, that I may be filled with joy, when I call to remembrance the genuine faith that is in you, which dwelt first in your grandmother Lois and your mother Eunice, and I am persuaded is in you also. Therefore, I remind you to stir up the Gift of God which is in you through the laying on of my hands."*

If we have a desire to stir up the Gifts of God, we must know 'What' we are stirring, 'Why' we are stirring, 'Where' we are going to stir, 'How' to go about doing so, and with 'Whom.' What does this mean? Simply put, we must take a look from within, based upon the teachings of our Forefathers, leaving no stone unturned; and once we find what we are looking for, we must be willing to SHARE, activating the Law of Reciprocity. How can we pinpoint them? Listed below are four Spiritual Woes we need to know, especially when dealing with the Gifts of the Spirit:

1. We must know the Gifts of God are from the same Spirit. We cannot mix and match good and evil; it is all good or evil. We cannot straddle the fence on this matter. If so, it is called a Deceptive Spirit. For this reason, we must understand, *"There are diversities of gifts, but the same Spirit."* 1 Corinthians 12:4. More importantly, we must know that confusing the two is indeed a Spiritual Woe. It says, *"Woe to those who call evil good, and good evil; who put darkness for light, and light for darkness; who put bitter for sweet, and sweet for bitter!"* Isaiah 5:20.

2. We must conclude that there are various ways to get through to God; for this reason, we must do what we are called to do. We must also leave the Holy Spirit's job up to Him and allow the Blood of Jesus to cover those who accept the covering. Here is what 1 Corinthians 12:5 says about varying ways: *"There are differences of ministries, but the same Lord."* Why do we need to know this? Frankly, this is another Spiritual Woe as well. According to Isaiah 5:21, here is what we must know: *"Woe to those who are wise in their own eyes, and prudent in their own sight!"*.

3. We must understand the Spirit works differently for each person based on our individuality, traumas, culture, or uniqueness. So, we cannot place ourselves or others in a box, especially within the confines of scripture. *"And there are diversities of activities, but it is the same God who works all in all."* 1 Corinthians 12:6. Nor can we hide from God, thinking we can get away with ungodly activities. *"Woe to those who seek deep to hide their counsel far from the LORD, and their works are in the dark; They say, 'Who sees us?' and, 'Who knows us?'"* Isaiah 29:15.

4. We cannot be selfish with the Gifts of the Spirit. When the Spirit calls upon it, we must proactively step into action. *"The manifestation of the Spirit is given to each one for the profit of all."* 1 Corinthians 12:7. When we use our Gifts, Calling, Creativity, and Talents selfishly, we put ourselves into a compromising position with the Holy of Holies. We are robbing those who need what we have to offer, and we are held accountable. Really? Yes, really! *"Woe to those who decree unrighteous decrees, who write misfortune, which they have prescribed to rob the needy of justice, and to take what is right from the poor of My people, that widows may be their prey, and that they may rob the fatherless."* Isaiah 10:1-2.

When truly walking in the Divine Gifts of the Spirit, Matthew 10:8 says, *"Freely you have received, freely give."* Not giving freely leads to one of the biggest Spiritual Woes of them all: DISOBEDIENCE. *"Woe to the rebellious children, says the LORD, who take counsel, but not of Me, and who devise plans, but not of My Spirit, that they may add sin to sin; who walk to go down to Egypt, and have not asked My advice, to strengthen themselves in the strength of Pharaoh, and to trust in the shadow of Egypt!"* Isaiah 30:1-2. From a Spiritual Perspective, this is how most of us zap our own Spiritual Gifts without realizing it, only to covet that of another.

Listen, most of our Spiritual Battles surround our Spiritual Gifts, the pouncing on those who proclaim to possess them, and the misuse of them for selfish reasons. Amid whatever or with whomever, we put on the Whole Armor of God, only to unawaringly fight against ourselves due to our lack of understanding of all things Spiritual.

If we are at war from within, we must resolve our inner battles first before contending with the wiles of the enemy to avoid cursing our hands. Why must we resolve inner conflict first? It prevents us from becoming yoked by self-induced tactics, prematurely revealing our rotten fruits or acts of coveting. Here is what the scripture says, *"Woe to those who devise iniquity, and work out evil on their beds! At morning light they practice it, because it is in the power of their hand. They covet fields and take them by violence, also houses, and seize them. So, they oppress a man and his house, a man and his inheritance."* Micah 2:1-2.

We can tiptoe around the Gifts of the Spirit, but when it comes down to the *Grandfather Clause*, we must use them to Spiritually Seal our Birthrights, *As It Pleases God*. What are the Gifts of the Spirit? They are:

1. The Word of Wisdom.
2. The Word of Knowledge.
3. The Gift of Faith.
4. The Gift of Healings.
5. The Working of Miracles.
6. The Gift of Prophecy.
7. The Discerning of Spirits.
8. Different Kinds of Tongues.
9. The Interpretation of Tongues.

The Ancient of Ancients wants us to know that the Heavenly of Heavens frown upon those who withhold to oppress, especially when it is within our power to give, help, or share with no strings attached. The more we use our Giftings, Calling, or Talents to give or to become a Blessing to others, the more we receive. Nevertheless, here is the scripture to align: *"For to one is given the word of wisdom through the Spirit, to another the word of knowledge through the same*

Spirit, to another faith by the same Spirit, to another gifts of healings by the same Spirit, to another the working of miracles, to another prophecy, to another discerning of spirits, to another different kinds of tongues, to another the interpretation of tongues. But one and the same Spirit works all these things, distributing to each one individually as He wills." 1 Corinthians 12:8-11.

According to the *Grandfather Clause* from the Heavenly of Heavens, if we want God's love, provision, and protection over our Divine Purpose, Birthrights, or Blueprint, we must confront the hidden quirks of our psyche. We can point the finger all we like, but once again, we all have quirks! Frankly, this is what makes us different, and it also contributes to our Purpose or Passion, linking us to our Divine Blueprint. In order for the enemy not to use our hidden quirks against us, we must know them, work on them, regraft them to a positive, perfect them, and then share them as our 'Give Back.'

Our weaknesses often harbor our Gifts, Calling, Talents, Creativity, and Purpose until we are ready to face what is already within. What does this mean? Our Divine Blueprint is already—the only person who determines its readiness is the one who possesses it. What about God? He placed the Tree of Life within us, and He will not violate our free wills. Thus, we as an individual must step *'Into the Spiritual Know'* about that which is already.

Just imagine if we think we have it going on right now without God. We will be astonished by what we can achieve with Him, being in Purpose on purpose, getting Divine Clarity, and solidifying our Spiritual Knowing *In Him.*

Chapter Eight

IN HIM

As the time is upon us to change, we are still at a standstill to which direction to take or which Blueprint to use. But unbeknown to most, regardless of where we are in life, reporting our findings concerning our Heaven on Earth Experience is sought after by the Kingdom of Heaven through the power of our TESTIMONY. We are a Spiritual Being having a human experience trapped in time, who have senses, emotions, and thoughts to govern the SEEDS and CYCLES set in motion from the inside out. If we fail to document or pay attention, we will tend to forget the vital DNA lineage linking us *In Him* by the Heavenly of Heavens.

When we operate and reflect wholeheartedly *In Him*, we will defy human logic and science with our Gifts, Calling, Talents, Purpose, Creativity, and Understanding. However, this Level of Spirituality is only achieved by a few, but secretly and openly sought after by all, even if we are in denial. How is this possible when we all have a unique Blueprint? We were born with the desire to dominate or have dominion, according to the Book of Genesis. *"So, God created man in His own image; in the image of God, He created him; male and female He created them. Then God blessed them, and God said to them, 'Be fruitful and multiply; fill the earth and subdue it; have dominion over the fish of the sea, over the birds of the air, and over every living thing that moves on the earth.' "* Genesis 1:27-28.

Yet, amid the time in which we live, we have become accustomed to dominating the wrong, worldly, or negative things, leaving ourselves open to the lack of proper self-governing. To add insult to injury, we most often do not have a clue we are in dire need of righteous, Kingdomly, or positive governing from the inside out, bringing us in Purpose on purpose.

Furthermore, as a *Word to the Wise*, by functioning in the Spirit of Excellence, it squashes the Spirit of Curiosity by default. Frankly, for those who do not know, ungoverned curiosity will cause us to experiment with everything or anyone without any form of Spiritual Discretion. However, for this Spiritual Journey, we must equip ourselves with the Spiritual Leverage needed to overcome evil with good. Why do we need to know this? In our own strength, our level of goodness is on a sliding scale of motives based upon the situation, circumstance, our understanding, or how we are feeling. If we do not use the Fruits of the Spirit and Christlike Character to govern the human psyche, we will find ourselves compromising without knowing we are doing so. Above all, it is still reflected in our heart postures in the Eye of God.

According to the Heavenly of Heavens, *In Him* is eulogized in our Heaven on Earth Experience, but for some reason, we have forgotten the Spiritual Protocol of the Kingdom. What does this mean? We are into ourselves and not into God, our Heavenly Father, as we should. Unfortunately, it could be resulting from our distractions, lack of understanding, unawareness on our behalf, conditioning, or from outright Spiritual Neglect. Who knows, besides the Spirit of God, right? Wrong, we know!

The Holy Spirit simply unveils that which is already. For this reason, we must stop playing pretend with ourselves, hoping or expecting someone to confirm or guide us on our journey through life, when the Blueprint is already written on the Tablet of the Heart.

As It Pleases God: Book Series

What is the big deal about *In Him*? *In Him* was derived from our Forefather Abraham, when pleading for his Bloodline, "*And the LORD said, 'Shall I hide from Abraham what I am doing, since Abraham shall surely become a great and mighty nation, and all the nations of the earth shall be blessed in him?*" Genesis 18:17-18. The bottom line is that we are not of our own accord; we are the lineage of something, and it is our responsibility to get *In Him*, to receive Divine Instructions similar to Abraham having the Three Visitors in Genesis 18. Now, if we fast forward this up to today's day and age from the Ancient of Days, we have what we know as the Holy Trinity (The Father, Son, and Holy Spirit) in Three Persons of the ONE that is *In Him*.

Unbeknown to most, *In Him* resides within us all, and we do not need to go seeking what is already. We must AWAKEN ourselves from our slumber, making a conscious effort to become a work-in-progress. In order to stay AWOKE, we must operate *In Him* with the Fruits of the Spirit and Christlike Character. What does this mean? *In Him* (In Jesus) is fed by good fruits, righteousness, and obedience.

In contrast, unrepentant or uncorrected rotten fruits, unrighteousness, and disobedience cause the Holy Spirit to lie dormant *In Him*. Meanwhile, deceptive Spirits take over, and we think we are operating *In Him* and we are NOT. How do we know the difference? Once again, we are known by our fruits!

How will operating *In Him* benefit us? When placing the Holy Trinity at the forefront of our lives, or better yet, by becoming Spiritually Awakened, covering ourselves with the Blood of Jesus, and making a conscious decision to operate *In Him*, here is the Spiritual Decree hidden in plain sight. "*Behold, I send an Angel before you to keep you in the way and to bring you into the place which I have prepared. Beware of Him and obey His voice; do not provoke Him, for He will not pardon your transgressions; for My name is in Him. But if you indeed obey His voice and do all that I speak, then I will be an enemy to your enemies and an adversary to your adversaries.*" Exodus 23:20-22.

We can discount the relevance of operating *In Him* all we like, but we should never judge what we do not understand. "*For You are my* lamp, O LORD; The LORD shall enlighten my darkness. For by You I can run against a troop; by my God I can leap over a wall. As for God, His way is perfect; the word of the LORD is proven; He is a shield to all who trust in Him. For who is God, except the LORD? And who is a rock, except our God? God is my strength and power, and He makes my way perfect. He makes my feet like the feet of deer, and sets me on my high places." 2 Samuel 22:29-34.

What is the Spiritual Contingency Clause for remaining *In Him*? No idolatry, period. Now, if idolatry or the idolators have a chokehold on us Mentally, Physically, and Emotionally, we must willfully break it from the inside out. Their sacred pillars become hidden in the human psyche; therefore, we must break them inwardly first, in order to see the manifestations outwardly. So, let us align this accordingly, *"You shall not bow down to their gods, nor serve them, nor do according to their works; but you shall utterly overthrow them and completely break down their sacred pillars. So, you shall serve the LORD your God, and He will bless your bread and your water. And I will take sickness away from the midst of you."* Exodus 23:24-25. Does this really work? Absolutely. Here is what the Bible says about Caleb, who operated in such a manner; *'But My servant Caleb, because he has a different spirit in him and has followed Me fully, I will bring into the land where he went, and his descendants shall inherit it."* Numbers 14:24.

We have all heard the abridged version of, 'In Him I live, and *In Him* I die,' right? But, according to scripture, it says, *"For in Him we live and move and have our being, as also some of your own poets have said, 'For we are also His offspring.' Therefore, since we are the offspring of God, we ought not to think that the Divine Nature is like gold or silver or stone, something shaped by art and man's devising. Truly, these times of ignorance God overlooked, but now commands all men everywhere to repent, because He has appointed a day on which He will judge the world in righteousness by the Man whom He has ordained. He has given assurance of this to all by raising Him from the dead."* Acts 17:28-31. All in all, this means we have to die to our fleshly or worldly ways, and walk in the Spirit of Righteousness, pray, repent, and delight *In Him* through Christ Jesus.

As It Pleases God: Book Series

God is on our side, even if we make a mistake, when we are falsely accused of wrongdoings, or when people are looking down on us based on our condition. Here is a scripture bringing hope to all, "*He shall pray to God, and He will delight in him, He shall see His face with joy, For He restores to man His righteousness. Then he looks at men and says, 'I have sinned, and perverted what was right, and it did not profit me.' He will redeem his soul from going down to the Pit, and his life shall see the light. Behold, God works all these things, Twice, in fact, three times with a man, to bring back his soul from the Pit, that he may be enlightened with the light of life.*" Job 33:26-30.

God is not expecting perfection; He expects obedience as we operate in the Spirit of Excellence. Is perfection and the Spirit of Excellence the same? No, they are not. In the Kingdom, perfection is being faultless and in need of no correction. The Spirit of Excellence is doing what it takes to get it right, build quality, develop durability, or create a win-win. Frankly, this is how we can operate *In Him*, amid our issues appearing real. What does this mean? What appears to be real to us is really based upon our perception. For this reason, *In Him* allows our Spiritual Eye to become opened, ushering in Divine Illumination for us to see the win-win, especially when others are seeing defeat.

Our Spiritual Ears are opened to hear the Voice of God and tame the unknown voices of deception as we develop our Spiritual Language from the Heavenly of Heavens. Yet, to the natural man, this sounds like a fairytale of some sort, but to the Spirit Man, it will resonate, quickening the human psyche. How can we make this make sense? For example, I am indeed writing *In Him*, under a full Kingdomly Commissioned Anointing. So, if the reader needs what this book is offering, the inner man, *Spirit to Spirit*, will willfully STAND at attention. Meanwhile, those for whom it is not for, will lack the understanding because their Spiritual Eye is not open to receive as of yet.

When truly operating *In Him*, it will change the trajectory of our lives, giving us the ability to manifest on a level that causes our enemies to scratch their heads in disbelief or stand in awe. The key is, when operating *In Him*, we do not need to make a public spectacle out of it. Should we not represent God? Of course, we should. Keep in mind that worldly representation is not the same as Kingdom Representation.

The Kingdom is looking for the Fruits of the Spirit and Christlike Character, NOT what comes out of our mouths or what we put on public display. We can say or do anything, masking our truth. In the interim, our fruits have their own language, speaking volumes without us having to say one word. When *In Him*, we must work on our fruits and character, like working a full-time job until we become well-versed in the Fruits of the Spirit and Christlike Character.

For the most part, we can look elsewhere for strength, but *In Him* resides what we need. Here is a scripture to keep close to the heart, *"The LORD is my strength and my shield; my heart trusted in Him, and I am helped; therefore, my heart greatly rejoices, and with my song I will praise Him. The LORD is their strength, and He is the saving refuge of His anointed."* Psalm 28:7-8.

What if the Vicissitudes of Life are pressing us to the max, and we do not know which way to turn? We must stand still for Divine Instructions while aligning ourselves with the Word of God, prayer, repentance, forgiveness, and positive affirmations. Once done, we can fervently say, *"Our soul waits for the LORD; He is our help and our shield. For our heart shall rejoice in Him, because we have trusted in His holy name."* Psalm 33:20-21.

Most often, when we are catching it from every angle, we feel compelled to do anything to make the pain or frustration go away. When, in all actuality, this is an indication that we need to get an understanding, period. Therefore, we do not need to engage in other things or with other people when we fail to understand the present situation, circumstance, events, or what is causing the uproar within our psyche.

Unbeknown to most, when we have an outward disturbance, it is really an inner disturbance manifesting itself outwardly to get our attention. Baloney, right? Wrong! Nothing makes it into the physical realm without having some form of Spiritual Manifestation first. And, if whatever it is was not connected to us from the inside out, we would not respond to it, nor would it provoke a reaction. Simply put, if we narrow down the inner SEED, we can deal with the outer manifestations provoking us to react, respond, or pay attention.

What if we are doing everything right, and things are still going wrong? If we are truthfully and faithfully operating *In Him*, while exhibiting the Fruits of the Spirit and Christlike Character with total humility and transparency, it often means that God is TESTING our patience, confidence, and staying power.

Why would God test us in this manner? Unfortunately, this is where most people give up, erecting a Golden Calf of idolatry, or they go to the dark side for the right now gratification. On the contrary, in the Kingdom, we must STAND on the Word of God without wavering, doing what we are called to do while being in Purpose on purpose, even if we are hurt, sick, traumatized, tattered, or torn.

If we stand for the Kingdom, *As It Pleases God*, without becoming divided, the Kingdom will have our backs, period. How will this benefit us amid oppression? We must view it as TRAINING for the next level of GREATNESS. Here are a few '*In Him*' pointers, but not limited to such:

1. *In Him*, we must not worry about those who plot wickedness. As long as we remain in a state of righteousness *In Him*, He has our backs, guaranteed! *"Do not fret because of evildoers, or be envious of the workers of iniquity. For they shall soon be cut down like the grass, and wither as the green herb."* Psalm 37:1-2.

2. *In Him*, we must trust Him, while doing everything in the Spirit of Excellence. *"Trust in the LORD, and do good; dwell in the land, and feed on His faithfulness."* Psalm 37:3.

3. *In Him*, we must enjoy being in His presence, building a *Spirit to Spirit* bond to place a Spiritual Seal on the Divine Relationship and the go-ahead on our Divine Blueprint. *"Delight yourself also in the LORD, and He shall give you the desires of your heart."* Psalm 37:4.

4. *In Him*, we must become committed to the Will of God regardless of the distractions or mishaps we encounter along the way. *"Commit your way to the LORD, trust also in Him, and He shall bring it to pass."* Psalm 37:5.

5. *In Him*, we must be ready, willing, and able to walk into our Divine Purpose when the timing is right or when we receive our Spiritual Cue. *"He shall bring forth your righteousness as the light, and your justice as the noonday."* Psalm 37:6.

6. *In Him*, we must NOT worry about the Dream Killers. Just rest *In Him*, knowing all things will work together for our good. *"Rest in the LORD, and wait patiently for Him; do not fret because of him who prospers in his way, because of the man who brings wicked schemes to pass."* Psalm 37:7.

7. *In Him*, we must NOT be overcome with anger, forgive, let go, and move on, bearing no grudges. *"Cease from anger, and forsake wrath; Do not fret—it only causes harm."* Psalm 37:8.

8. *In Him*, we must be patient. *"For evildoers shall be cut off; But those who wait on the LORD, they shall inherit the earth."* Psalm 37:9.

9. *In Him* will cause our issues to vanish away like vapors when we least expect it. *"For yet a little while and the wicked shall be no more; Indeed, you will look carefully for his place, but it shall be no more."* Psalm 37:10.

10. *In Him*, meekness will cause us to abound in a state of peacefulness, superseding human understanding: *"But the meek shall inherit the earth, and shall delight themselves in the abundance of peace."* Psalm 37:11.

11. *In Him*, ushers in the day of reckoning for those who spitefully attempt to wreak havoc in our lives. *"The wicked plots against the just, and gnashes at him with his teeth. The Lord laughs at him, for He sees that his day is coming."* Psalm 37:12-13.

12. *In Him*, when we are content with what we have, while operating in the Spirit of Righteousness, He will cause the weapons of warfare to ricochet, or He will outright deflect them from the intended target. *"The wicked have drawn the sword and have bent their bow, to cast down the poor and needy, to slay those who are of upright conduct. Their sword shall enter their own heart, and their bows shall be broken. A little that a righteous man has, is better than the riches of many wicked."* Psalm 37:14-16.

Regardless of where we are in life or what we have been through, we are safe *In Him*; we only need to trust *In Him* and the process it takes to extract the Greatness from Within. *"For You will light my lamp; the LORD my God will enlighten my darkness. For by You I can run against a troop, by my God I can leap over a wall. As for God, His way is perfect; the word of the LORD is proven; He is a shield to all who trust in Him. For who is God, except the LORD? And who is a rock, except our God? It is God who arms me with strength, and makes my way perfect."* Psalm 18:28-32.

Chapter Nine

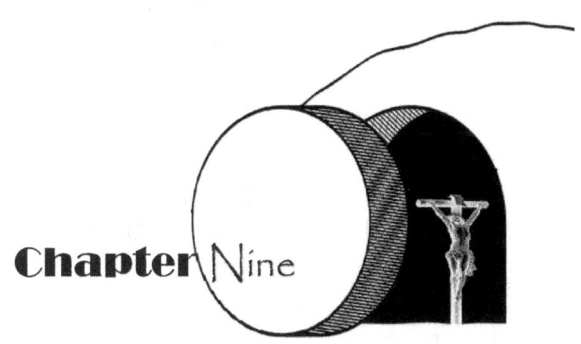

PERCEPTIONAL WORTHINESS

The notion of *Perceptional Worthiness* has been swept under the rug long enough; it has been walked upon for too long, and now is the time to pull it from underneath the rug. Having a *Worthwhile Perception* is the way to enhance a sense of value from the inside out. Yet, only a few of us have taken the time to enhance this invaluable commodity, which has the potential to offset any form of defeat. Better yet, it allows us to create a win-win out of the most challenging situations, regardless of our deed, creed, or breed.

As we pull back the curtains of life, we must know that our outlook is based upon our inlook (view from within). What does this mean? How we see ourselves from within determines how we perceive life, even if we have been conditioned to behave, react, or communicate a certain way. Though we can mask our perception, the moment we are placed under pressure, what is within comes out. How is this possible, especially when our self-control is up to par? First and foremost, we are not robots. We are human beings having the ability to deal with people, places, and things Mentally, Physically, Emotionally, and Spiritually.

As It Pleases God®: Book Series

Now, with these four abilities, we are able to step into action, freeze up, go into hiding, go into fight mode, go into negative habit-forming mode to cope, break down, act a fool, remain calm, plead the fifth, and so on. As a result, we must become cautious in all of our sayings, doings, and becoming.   It may cause Spiritual Blindness, Deafness, or Muteness, depending upon our motives.

To maximize our *Perceptional Worthiness*, it is imperative to clear our Spiritual Vision, unclog our Spiritual Ears, and develop our Spiritual Language from the Heavenly of Heavens. By doing so, our perception will begin to merge with the Heavenly Perception of the Kingdom to eventually become ONE. However, to complete the merging process, we must Spiritually See, Hear, and Speak clearly without having worldly static clouding our sense of good judgment.

Believe it or not, our survival instincts are predicated on our perception, determining what we will or will not do to sustain life as we see it from a Worldly or Kingdom Perspective. What is the difference? Listed below are a few examples, but not limited to such:

Worldly Perspective:

1. The phrase: '*By any means necessary*' is based upon our perception.
2. The phrase: '*Get them before they get me*' is based upon our perception.
3. The phrase: '*My way or no way*' is based upon our perception.
4. The phrase: '*Whatever it takes*' is based upon our perception.
5. The phrase: '*Everything is about me*' is based upon our perception.
6. The phrase: '*What is mine is mine*' is based upon our perception.
7. The phrase: '*Any cup is mine as long as I have one*' is based upon our perception.
8. The phrase: '*Me, Me, Me*' is based upon our perception.
9. The phrase: '*I always get my way*' is based upon our perception.

10. The phrase: *'I will fight until the end'* is based upon our perception.
11. The phrase: *'I have tricks in my bag'* or *'I have tricks up my sleeve'* is based upon our perception.
12. The phrase: *'My god is better than yours'* or *'I am the god over my own life'* is based upon our perception.

Clearly, we have the free will to believe what we so desire, yet all of the above statements can become negative or positive based on our perception. As we synergize from the Heavenly of Heavens, by changing the trajectory of how we think, we can open up the Gates of Heaven on our behalf. Really? Yes, really! When it comes down to our perception, if we intertwine the Divine Synergy of the Kingdom, we empower ourselves by default.

At first, it may feel a little weird, but once we become accustomed to having a Kingdom Mindset, it will trump anything known to man, breaking Spiritual Blindness, Deafness, and Muteness to the core. Plus, it shatters negative, deflective mirrors designed to rehash our past to blind our future. Really? Yes, really! Listed below are a few examples, but not limited to such:

Kingdom Perspective:

1. The expression: *'By any means necessary according to the Will of God'* is based upon our Kingdom Perception.
2. The expression: *'Let me put on the Whole Armor of God before they attack me'* is based upon our Kingdom Perception.
3. The expression: *'God's way or no way'* is based upon our Kingdom Perception.
4. The expression: *'Whatever it takes to allow God's Will to be done or As It Pleases Him'* is based upon our Kingdom Perception.
5. The expression: *'Everything is about the Kingdom according to my Divine Blueprint'* is based upon our Kingdom Perception.

6. The expression: 'What belongs to me is already according to my Divine Blueprint' is based upon our Kingdom Perception.
7. The expression: 'My cup runneth over according to my Divine Blueprint' is based upon our Kingdom Perception.
8. The expression: 'It is between Us and Them' or 'We are ONE' is based upon our Kingdom Perception.
9. The expression: 'The Will of God must be fulfilled according to my Divine Blueprint' is based upon our Kingdom Perception.
10. The expression: 'The Fight is Finished' or 'God has already provided' is based upon our Kingdom Perception.
11. The expression: 'No weapon formed against me shall prosper' is based upon our Kingdom Perception.
12. The expression: 'My God, which art in Heaven is my Way, my Truth, and my Life' or 'My God provides my daily Bread according to His riches and glory in Christ Jesus' is based upon our Kingdom Perception.

When we redirect our wants, needs, and desires back to the Kingdom to affirm our STAND or as a positive affirmation, we allow our plans to have an opportunity to become corrected, redirected, regrafted, or adjusted according to our Divine Blueprint. Why are adjustments necessary? First, God did not create us as robots; He wants us involved as relational beings. Secondly, He does not give us all the details upfront because we have to want whatever He has in mind, *As It Pleases Him*, while developing our focus. As a word of caution, if we are constantly consumed with distractions without setting some form of Spiritual Guards or Limitations, we may NOT be ready to be in Purpose on purpose as of yet. Thirdly, it also trains our Spiritual Muscles to instinctively know what is for us and what is not, based on our internal components through our senses, instincts, or conscience.

In moving forward in our *Perceptional Worthiness*, we must put away our selfishness, pride, coveting, competitiveness, jealousy, envy, or greed to get our full portion. Unbeknown to most, while in or out of the Will of God, we are often operating on a fraction or a portion of our Divine Blueprint. In my opinion, this is similar to a faucet leaking or dripping water, and to get it to flow fully, we must increase the pressure.

Now, this fraction depends upon us, on the timing, the amount of training required, the appropriate season, the amount of healing needed, the level of trauma endured, and so on. Fortunately, or unfortunately for some, this is why we feel a void, longing, internal drive, or tugging from within, letting us know there is MORE. Yet, due to our lack of understanding, we are unable to figure out what is wrong or why we are feeling the way we do. So, we suppress it, hoping we will have an 'Aha' moment. Well, this is it! That 'Aha' moment has come and is NOW!

Our *Perceptional Worthiness* or Positive Mental Mindset depends upon us to have a want, work for, or place a demand on it. Simply put, we are waiting for the 'Aha' moment, but it is already prewired into our DNA. Yes, it is already in our system; we just need to become AWARE of it to unveil it. Unfortunately, it is hidden under layers of negative debris; therefore, we must do a clean sweep of all negative characteristics, behaviors, thoughts, actions, desires, habits, and so on. When doing so, do not worry about the residue left behind. What if we have a real mess? First, we have the Holy Spirit to help in the clean-up process to correct the correctable through the Fruits of the Spirit and Christlike Character. Secondly, we have the Blood of Jesus to cover the menial quirks we have through our ability to pray, repent, and fast on occasion to enforce the Heavenly Contract of grace, mercy, and forgiveness.

By reinforcing our lives with the Word of God and positive affirmations, we can steer our lives back to the right path, mainly when we get off course, lost, distracted, distressed, or confused. What is the right path? Regardless of how we attempt to complicate life, there are only two paths leading to all things or any form of pitstop along the way, which are:

1. The Path of Righteousness.
2. The Path of Unrighteousness.

As It Pleases God®: Book Series

Keeping the Kingdom uncomplicated can quickly streamline our character into good or bad, right or wrong, just or unjust, positive or negative, without anyone calling us out or pointing the finger. We do not need anyone to tell us when we are right or wrong; we already know! However, the complications come into play when we attempt to rationalize or justify whatever or with whomever.

Querying ourselves with a self-analysis or self-mirror of righteousness vs. unrighteousness will help us in ways beyond human understanding while automatically putting our human psyche in self-correct mode. Once the psyche is trained to become ONE with the Holy Spirit, due to our Spiritual Awareness, if it knows it is right, our conscience will peacefully move forward. If it is wrong, our conscience will kick in, and it is questioned in the *What, When, Where, Why, How,* and with *Whom* formation. And, being that the human psyche does not like to be questioned constantly, it will do the right thing naturally, putting our conscience on high alert to avoid being called out.

Unbeknown to most, the human psyche does not like to be put on display for corrective action to occur, nor does it like any red flags to alert the Holy Spirit of miscalculations or misdirection. For this reason, when delving into any known or unknown unrighteousness, it will seek to control us Mentally, Physically, and Emotionally by any means necessary while negatively governing our thoughts, emotions, feelings, perception, and so on, similar to having a temper tantrum.

To add insult to injury, when we become Spiritually Blind, Deaf, or Mute, the negative will appear positive. How is this possible? Frankly, this is when we think we are right in our own eyes or in denial, but all so wrong in the Eye of God based upon our fruits or characteristics. What does this mean? It simply means that we went about doing something the wrong way, or our intentions were unrighteous. For this reason, it is best to query ourselves with the Fruits of the Spirit in or out of our moments of unsurety.

More importantly, once the thermostat of our psyche is set on righteousness, *As It Pleases God*, it governs our motives to ensure the gauge is set correctly, even amid hiccups woven into our daily living. For example, even if something wrong happens based upon the erring of another, a mistake of uncommonness happens, when our worthiness is underhandedly being tested, or we are intentionally set up to err to bring shame to our names. Despite being in this state, if our intentions were righteous, we would not be penalized severely for any wrongdoings due to having the correct and sincere heart posture, *As It Pleases Him*.

Do we get a free pass? Unfortunately, this is not my call. The level of Divine Grace and Mercy and free passes are between God, the offender, and the offendee. Moreover, we do not know what He is using to train, mold, or provoke us. Clearly, there are times when we can set the record straight when such a hiccup happens, but there are times when we must leave well enough alone while continuing to move forward in the Spirit of Righteousness and Excellence, *As It Pleases Him*.

In the Union of Oneness, it is imperative to understand that we are a Vessel of God, regardless of how we feel about our relationship with Him, our past mistakes, the issues we are facing, and so on. However, our *Perceptional Worthiness* positions us to embrace our Divine Blueprint according to our Heavenly Intents of being in Purpose on purpose.

According to the Heavenly of Heavens, we must prove and establish our worthiness based on our actions, reactions, desires, motives, character, and willingness. We cannot do whatever we want, whenever we desire, however we decide, and with whomever, without accounting for the cost positively or negatively. So, it behooves us to take responsibility without becoming reckless Mentally, Physically, Emotionally, or Spiritually. What does recklessness have to do with our *Perceptional Worthiness*? Recklessness has Spiritual Repercussions, bringing about yokes, bondages, generational curses, or the Wrath of God. For example:

- *Mental Recklessness* causes us to entertain all types of thoughts, producing false truths or narratives without having factual information. In the Kingdom, we cannot allow the Mind to run wild, doing whatever it wants without placing restraints. The enemy's playground resides in the Mind of an ungoverned vestibule of negative chatter, manifesting itself into the physical realm in due time. Unbeknown to most, our thoughts are SEEDS, affecting our emotions and sprouting up in the physical realm in due season.

- *Emotional Recklessness* causes us to become stuck in our feelings, harbor unforgiveness, indulge in hatefulness, cause confusion, spread gossip, create chaos, or hurt others for no apparent reason. It also incorporates any negative feelings, causing our psyche to traumatize us or others without any form of restraint. At the same time, we allow ourselves to carry on with negative antics relating to envy, jealousy, pride, greed, coveting, hatefulness, rudeness, and so on. The bottom line is that this is the absence of the Fruits of the Spirit and Christlike Character, whether it is long-term or short-term. Regardless of our intentions, it will make its way into the physical realm as an explosion or implosion, especially when left uncorrected and unrepentant.

- *Physical Recklessness* causes us to indulge in the lust of the eyes, the lust of the flesh, and the pride of life, which consumes our senses, habits, and fruits. Frankly, this is often noticed in our actions, reactions, what proceeds out of the gateway of the mouth, our charactorial traits, our outward behaviors, how we treat others, our level of proactiveness, or any form of negative outward manifestation of *Mental* and *Emotional Recklessness*. Above all, it will also appear in our soul ties caused by promiscuousness.

- *Spiritual Recklessness* causes us to use the Word of God to dethrone others instead of building them up. It will also contribute to us becoming a wolf in sheep's clothing, a Spiritual Pimp, or a master manipulator, cursing people, misusing scripture as a form of witchcraft, or creating all types of negative manifestations using Spirituality to cause unjustified harm to the innocent. In addition, with all the other unrepentant and uncorrected forms of recklessness, it will cause the Holy Spirit to lie dormant, especially when disobedience or arrogance is involved.

With all due respect, some preach we do not have to do anything to be in the Will of God or to pursue Purpose, but this is the biggest form of deception known to man. From a Spiritual Perspective, this is like telling us that we do not need a SEED to reproduce or oxygen to live.

Listen to me, and listen to me well, according to the Cycle of Life, there must be a TRIGGER of a SEED to receive the proper instructions causing growth, movement, or reaction. If there is no trigger or provocation of some sort, there is no reaction or a jumpstart for the Law of Causation. Without some form of action, it contributes to stagnancy, death, or some form of phantom symptom of falseness, deception, masks, or a false sense of self-worth.

According to the Heavenly of Heavens, being that fakeness does not have a seedful trigger of growth or maturity, the Cycle of Life will return whatever it is back to the earth by taking out the weakest, unproductive link. Why is fakeness not a growth trigger? Fakeness is manmade and cannot be reproduced naturally without the help of the originator who created the synthesis. Inopportunely, this is why we get a lot of individuals faking their Spiritual Astuteness, creating an illusion for onlookers. Once the mask is removed, they are exhausted or fall into a state of depression instantly. How can we resolve this? Do not pretend! In the Kingdom, transparency is a must, and if something is fake, admit it!

As It Pleases God®: Book Series

Building Kingdom Authenticity is best done by looking and tilling for the Seed, Trigger, or Susceptibility hidden in our Gifts, Talents, Calling, or Creativity. What does all of this mean for us in layman's terms? Based upon the Spiritual Decree set forth in the Garden of Eden, mainly with the Adam and Eve Experience in the Book of Genesis, we must put in the work, becoming a work-in-progress from the inside out. How do we make this make sense? The Seed or Trigger will reside in something or someone. Now, for our *Perceptional Worthiness*, we must take out the shovel and dig deep within the human psyche to extract the Divine Treasures we possess, which are hidden in a weakness, vice, habit, or the negative. From experience, this is accomplished by tilling it until it becomes a win-win or a positive manifestation without settling for defeat or deception.

How do we Spiritually Till? Spiritually Tilling our own ground is accomplished by asking the right fact-finding questions in the *What, When, Where, Why, How*, and with *Whom* formation to become better at whatever or with whomever. We must also learn, train, understand, educate ourselves, and document consistently, taking notes without fail. What is the purpose of going through this process for a weakness? Our Divine Fruitfulness or Provision will most often reside in a Seed that must be broken, nurtured, and watered to produce. In addition, it also teaches gratefulness, gives us experience, develops obedience, and helps us become merciful, compassionate, forgiving, and understanding.

In establishing our *Perceptional Worthiness*, by missing the developmental process or refusing to put in the work, we deprive ourselves of specific lessons, experiences, cleansing, or uprooting that can only come from us. What does this mean? Everyone is different, having different issues, traumas, and upsets in need of regrafting, making our weaknesses our greatest strengths; therefore, we have to work on this for ourselves. Unfortunately, no one can stand in proxy for us; we must put in the work. To be clear, we can have someone help or pinpoint the area needing reckoning, but the '*sweat of our brow*' must come from us.

For example, if I refused to listen, learn, understand, regraft, uproot, prune, cast down, usher in, take notes, and so on, I would not be able to write on this Spiritual Level with such conviction, clarity, and astuteness. Although my Spiritual Journey was not easy, and I would not wish this upon my worst enemy, it was necessary for my Commissioning Process for such a time as this.

With outright humility, I do not pull any punches, nor do I back down from doing what I have been called to do, regardless of the opinionated thoughts or biases of others. I respect the fact that everyone is entitled to their opinion. If they are not receiving Divine Instructions from the Heavenly of Heavens, then their time is being misgoverned in some way, which means deception is amid the opinion.

I am here to provide Spiritual Understanding, Tools, How-To, and Know-How to build the Kingdom of Heaven, *As It Pleases God*. Thus, I cannot put in the work for anyone or change their opinionated thoughts. So, in order to stay focused and gather the necessary information to help those who are willing to put in the work to help themselves, I will ILLUMINATE the way, guiding them toward the Light without violating their free will.

In the Eye of God, the *Tilling Process* is up to us, especially if we want to maximize our Gifts, Calling, Talents, Creativity, or Purpose. If we choose not to, then we cannot lay the blame elsewhere, and we have no right to become jealous, envious, or covet another person who makes it their business to put in the work to till their Fields of Greatness. Do we not have free will to do whatever we like? Yes, we do, but exhibiting this sort of negative behavior to someone who is putting in the work will cause God to allow the Vicissitudes of Life to smite us, tossing us to and fro.

In my opinion, if we want to exhibit negative behaviors or characteristics, we should exhibit them around those who are in the same category of negativity. What is the purpose of doing so? Negative plus negative equals negative; therefore, if we wallow with our equal, then the Spiritual Penalties are much less because both are in AGREEMENT.

On the other hand, suppose we exhibit negative fruits or characteristics to unjustifiably afflict the person who is putting in the work from the inside out, doing the Will of God, *As It Pleases Him*. In this case, we will become the ENEMY of God. The two are not in AGREEMENT, creating conflicting vibes. Then again, if they are operating in the Spirit of Righteousness with the Fruits of the Spirit and Christlike Character, *As It Pleases Him*, we will inadvertently create a ditch for ourselves as well. Blasphemy, right? Unfortunately, wrong again.

Spiritual Cluelessness is how we get caught up, becoming yoked, or we unawaringly create generational curses, affecting our Bloodline. Please allow me to align this accordingly: *"Behold, the wicked brings forth iniquity; Yes, he conceives trouble and brings forth falsehood. He made a pit and dug it out, and has fallen into the ditch which he made. His trouble shall return upon his own head, and his violent dealing shall come down on his own crown. I will praise the LORD according to His righteousness, and will sing praise to the name of the LORD Most High."* Psalm 7:14-17.

Our *Perceptional Worthiness* is not predicated on taking the easy way out, opting to pass the buck, or blocking those who are in Purpose on purpose. We have stored information within the human psyche that we need to gain access to, and we need the Holy Spirit to do so. Why do we need Him? We need experience and understanding about ourselves, insight into righteousness, and access to the Divine Mysteries associated with our Divine Blueprint or our Heaven on Earth Experiences. Plus, with His guidance, we can boldly walk in the Spirit and in Truth with no regrets and *As It Pleases God*.

On the other hand, if we opt to remain Spiritually Asleep, we become limited, subjecting ourselves to Spiritual Ignorance or Deprivation. How is this possible, especially when we are sitting pretty? Regardless of what we think, how much we have accomplished, our status, or whatever is associated with our worldly means of operation, without the Holy Trinity, we subject ourselves to psychological invasion. How? We will become consumed from within with the lust of the eyes, the lust of the flesh, and the pride of life, leading to chaos, negativity, ungratefulness, jealousy, pride, envy, coveting, debauchery, and so on.

Now, let us take this a step further: If we decide NOT to walk in our Giftings, Calling, Talents, or Creativity, we simply prolong the process until we eventually surrender. What does this mean? We inadvertently kick-start the Cycle of Déjà vu instead of the Cycle of Change according to our Divine Blueprint. In my opinion, repeating the same cycle over and over is exhausting and time-consuming, especially when it takes the same amount of energy or less to unveil our authentic selves.

When it comes down to our Divine Blueprint or our *Perceptional Worthiness*, we are indeed geniuses in this area. Still, it cannot come forth if we do not surrender to it, or we become distracted by killing the dreams of others. No matter where we are at this stage, all is not lost if we work diligently on the Fruits of the Spirit and building Christlike Character. By doing so in the Spirit of Excellence and Righteousness, there is no limit on what we can achieve, nor can anyone put a cap on our Level of Impact. Really? Yes, really!

Unbeknown to most, when we surrender to our Divine Blueprint, the Floodgates of Wisdom will yield on our behalf and that of our Bloodline, guaranteed! Therefore, once we align ourselves accordingly, we will no longer have to question our worthiness; it becomes established in the Kingdom among the Heavenly of Heavens.

All of our Spiritual Resources from the Heavenly of Heavens are properly positioned to complete the Mission of the Kingdom, period! As a word of caution, once we get to this Spiritual Level, we are the only person who can hinder this process. For this reason, we must MAKE SURE of a few things, but not limited to such:

1. Make sure the Holy Trinity is at the forefront of our lives.
2. Make sure that our Fruits of the Spirit are up to par.
3. Make sure that our Christlike Character is coming forth as pure gold.

4. Make sure we are a work-in-progress in a constant State of Repentance.
5. Make sure we give thanks in all things while creating a win-win out of everything with a Positive Mental Mindset.
6. Make sure we document our *Spirit to Spirit* Encounters.
7. Make sure we forgive with no strings attached.
8. Make sure we remain calm.
9. Make sure we share.
10. Make sure we govern our tongues.
11. Make sure we cancel negative thoughts, words, emotions, or desires.
12. Make sure we approach everything, *As It Pleases God*.

Lastly, if we do not limit ourselves to the earthly realm, we become Spiritually Unstoppable in our Heaven on Earth Experience. So, today marks a new beginning. Pick up your CROWN, and grow GREAT!

www.DrYBur.com

Chapter Ten

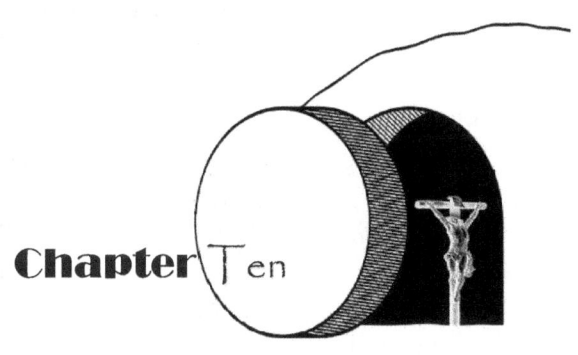

HEAVENLY PERSPECTIVE

The desired *Heavenly Perspective* we should have is not often thought of in such a manner. We often think Heaven is an illusion when, in all actuality, it is indeed reversed. We are the illusion appearing lifelike, and Heaven is real, appearing as an illusion. How do we make this make sense, especially when we can clearly see ourselves and are clueless about this Heavenly stuff? Just because we cannot see the manifestations of the Spirit with our naked eyes does not mean it is not real. Therefore, we must elevate ourselves to understand that the unseen is indeed more powerful than the seen.

Without having a thought first, nothing makes its way into reality, period! Yet, let us go to the Book of Genesis to establish how our Heavenly System works: *"In the beginning God created the heavens and the earth."* Genesis 1:1. What does this have to do with us? This scripture established Who was here first, ensuring we do not get the creative efforts that followed suit confused.

To take this a step further, Genesis 1:2 says, *"The earth was without form, and void; and darkness was on the face of the deep. And the Spirit of God was hovering over the face of the waters."* The moment we forget Who is in charge, we will naturally revert to some form of deformation, void, darkness, or thirst within the human psyche. Keep in mind that the Spirit of God is living and moving throughout, regardless of whether we admit it or not.

Amazingly, the minute we think we have God cornered, He will illuminate the areas in need of Light. Really? Yes, really. *"Then God said, 'Let there be light;' and there was light. And God saw the light, that it was good; and God divided the light from the darkness."* Genesis 1:3-4. Frankly, it is God who allows the Light to shine through us, eliminating darkness; therefore, we should never become ungrateful for the simple things in life.

Now, with all due respect, for those who do not believe in the Bible, it is okay. Why is this okay? The Word of God is designed to make a believer out of us. Listen, what God sets in motion will do what it is designed to do, regardless of what we think, feel, believe, or attempt to stop.

What God says it is, so shall it be. For example, *"God called the light Day, and the darkness He called Night. So, the evening and the morning were the first day."* Genesis 1:5. No one can change this one fact, which means the Spiritual Principles designed to govern our experiences in life will not change; they are ABSOLUTE, making it important to understand people, places, and things from a *Heavenly Perspective*. Once we know and understand God's Divine Intent, we are better able to respectfully and humbly approach Him without doing so amissly.

For this reason, the goal of this chapter is to regraft the MINDSET from worldly to Spiritual, based upon the *Heavenly Perspective* set in motion from the Ancient of Days. What can this do for us? It brings us into the Spiritual Light, granting us Divine Understanding and Wisdom unlike any other.

For example, when people begin to question the authenticity of our abilities, or when they begin seeking us out, saying something similar to, *"There is a man in your Kingdom in whom is the Spirit of the Holy God. And in the days of your father, light and understanding and wisdom, like the wisdom of the gods, were found in him."* Daniel 5:11A. What are we able to do in this state of being, mainly when the Spirit of God is upon us? According to Daniel's experience, "*Inasmuch as an excellent spirit, knowledge, understanding, interpreting dreams, solving riddles, and explaining enigmas were found in this Daniel, whom the king named Belteshazzar, now let Daniel be called, and he will give the interpretation.*"

Clearly, this is all at the discretion of the Holy Spirit based upon our *Heavenly Perspective*. If our Spiritual Perspective is off-key, then our interpretation will be off as well; therefore, the Spirit of God will withhold information until we clear our Spiritual Channels, *As It Pleases Him*. Is this fair? Absolutely. We cannot afford to get it wrong in His Name, especially when we have the same opportunity to get it RIGHT!

What gives us the same opportunity to get it right, specifically when we are all different? First, we must know our STAND with the Holy Trinity. Secondly, the Spirit of God will not Spiritually Commission us where we are not Gifted. Thirdly, when we are One with the Spirit of God, we will know our Unction to Function; in so many words, we will know *What, When, Where, How, Why,* and with *Whom* our oil flows. If it does not flow, we must question it!

According to the *Heavenly of Heavens*, we must unpack what we have learned from a worldly perspective to truly absorb the training needed to approach life from God's Perspective. How is this possible when our Heaven on Earth Experience is staring us right in the face? Our experiences work best when we pride ourselves on using the Spiritual Principles already set in place. At the same time, utilizing the Fruits of the Spirit and Christlike Character consistently without fail, or becoming wishy-washy.

My ear has been to the ground long enough to hear those proclaiming Holiness, and their attitude, behaviors, character, and demeanor represent a mirror image of unrighteousness while thinking they are righteous and justified. Yet, they have a trail of rotten fruits, traumatized victims, unmended bridges, hateful actions, broken relationships, a history of debauchery, and so on. If one has not experienced this yet, just live a little longer.

As we take this a step further, the Heavenly of Heaven's call to action is designed to awaken us from our Spiritual Slumber. How do we know when we are Spiritually Awakened? When we take the focus off of ourselves, placing it on the Will of God and our Divine Blueprint, *As It Pleases Him*, we will know the change has occurred.

As long as selfishness is clouding our sense of good judgment, we still have work to do. Selfishness does not make us bad people; it simply means we must do a little more work to unravel the worldly knots that have us entangled in a web of deception. What is the quickest way to break selfishness? From a Heavenly Perspective, we must become genuinely humble and loving. Really? Yes, really!

Most think that prayer alone breaks selfishness, but it does not! Selfish praying exists in those lacking humility and those operating in a disobedient heart posture. Humility helps us to obtain our Birthrights and Blessings without having shame or ungratefulness attached. Bringing shame to the Kingdom due to some form of recklessness, negligence, debauchery, or ungratefulness are a few ways to become detached from the Holy Spirit, causing Him to go into a state of dormancy until we come to ourselves.

Can the Holy Spirit depart from us? Of course. God will allow His Spirit to depart while allowing a distressing one to take His place, primarily when we are in a state of willful disobedience. In addition, this will also happen when we begin to use Him as a form of manipulative leverage to get what we want, or when we outright pimp Him out, similar to the King Saul experience in 1 Samuel 15 and 16.

Now, on the other hand, He will come upon us to intervene as well, preventing us from destroying ourselves or His Chosen Vessels of Conveyance. By far, this is similar to how the Spirit of God came upon Balaam in Numbers 24:1-2. *"Now when Balaam saw that it pleased the LORD to bless Israel, he did not go as at other times, to seek to use sorcery, but he set his face toward the wilderness. And Balaam raised his eyes, and saw Israel encamped according to their tribes; and the Spirit of God came upon him."*

How do we begin to operate with a *Heavenly Perspective* while having the Holy Spirit remain in our favor? We must begin with RESPECT for God's Divine Order, *As It Pleases Him*. When we disrespect it, we will begin to digress in receiving respect; therefore, we have to use other means of appearing as if we are respectful or deserve it. Listed below are a few items to Respect, but not limited to such:

1. Respect our Creator. He is the Beginning and the End; therefore, we are somewhere in between, so respect the process of Divine Conveyance. *"In the beginning God created the heavens and the earth. The earth was without form, and void; and darkness was on the face of the deep. And the Spirit of God was hovering over the face of the waters."* Genesis 1:1-2.

2. Respect the Light and Darkness and the timetable governing it. Therefore, we should give thanks for both because they create balance and understanding, allowing us to know and experience the difference between them. In addition, it gives us a way to measure our days based upon a simulation of the light of day and the dark of night, depending upon where we are located. And, regardless of where we are, it provides a 24-hour inclusive timetable of measurement. *"And God saw the light, that it was good; and God divided the light from the darkness. God called the light Day, and the darkness He called Night. So, the evening and the morning were the first day."* Genesis 1:4-5.

3. Respect the Universal Laws set in motion, putting everything in their proper perspective. For example, the Laws of Gravity keep us pulled to the Earth's core, ensuring we do not float around from pillar to post. Although this does not include the Higher Laws, it is one that we can all understand and relate to outside of the Laws governing the travel of Light and Sound or the Law of Oneness, Energy, Action, Cause and Effect, Reciprocity, Attraction, Correspondence, Relativity, Polarity, Rhythm, and so on. The key is to RESPECT them all. *"Then God said, 'Let there be a firmament in the midst of the waters, and let it divide the waters from*

the waters.' Thus, God made the firmament, and divided the waters which were under the firmament from the waters which were above the firmament; and it was so. And God called the firmament Heaven. So, the evening and the morning were the second day." Genesis 1:6-8.

4. Respect the elements of water because it is indeed a sustaining force to life and the cleansing process therein. "Then God said, Let the waters under the heavens be gathered together into one place, and let the dry land appear; and it was so. And God called the dry land Earth, and the gathering together of the waters He called Seas. And God saw that it was good." Genesis 1:9-10.

5. Respect the SEEDS and FRUITS of all things, knowing that Seedtime and Harvest will produce after their own kind. "Then God said, Let the earth bring forth grass, the herb that yields seed, and the fruit tree that yields fruit according to its kind, whose seed is in itself, on the earth; and it was so. And the earth brought forth grass, the herb that yields seed according to its kind, and the tree that yields fruit, whose seed is in itself according to its kind. And God saw that it was good." Genesis 1:11-12.

6. Respect the Season we are in or the Season of another. We must also respect Mother Nature, even if we do not understand what is going on. It is designed to take care of itself and us, especially when we develop a bond with it, knowing that it is designed to serve us as we do our part in protecting it. "Then God said, Let there be lights in the firmament of the heavens to divide the day from the night; and let them be for signs and seasons, and for days and years; and let them be for lights in the firmament of the heavens to give light on the earth; and it was so." Genesis 1:14-15.

7. Respect the Greater and Lesser Lights, good and evil, right and wrong, just and unjust, and so on. Spiritual Duality is the process of regrafting and restoration; plus, it brings

everything into or out of BALANCE in due time, according to the Will of God. "Then God made two great lights: the greater light to rule the day, and the lesser light to rule the night. He made the stars also. God set them in the firmament of the heavens to give light on the earth, and to rule over the day and over the night, and to divide the light from the darkness. And God saw that it was good." Genesis 1:16-18.

8. Respect Nature as they do what it is called to do, reproducing after its own kind. "Then God said, 'Let the waters abound with an abundance of living creatures, and let birds fly above the earth across the face of the firmament of the heavens.' So, God created great sea creatures and every living thing that moves, with which the waters abounded, according to their kind, and every winged bird according to its kind. And God saw that it was good. And God blessed them, saying, 'Be fruitful and multiply, and fill the waters in the seas, and let birds multiply on the earth.' " Genesis 1:20-22.

9. Respect Animals. Every animal serves a purpose, regardless of whether we understand them or not. Or, whether they creep us out, they still have a Divine Role to play according to their Blueprint. "Then God said, 'Let the earth bring forth the living creature according to its kind: cattle and creeping thing and beast of the earth, each according to its kind;' and it was so. And God made the beast of the earth according to its kind, cattle according to its kind, and everything that creeps on the earth according to its kind. And God saw that it was good." Genesis 1:24-25.

10. Respect all Human Life. "Then God said, 'Let Us make man in Our image, according to Our likeness; let them have dominion over the fish of the sea, over the birds of the air, and over the cattle, over all the earth and over every creeping thing that creeps on the earth.' So, God created man in His own image; in the image of God, He created him; male and female He created them." Genesis 1:26-27.

11. Respect the Giftings, Calling, Talents, Creativity, and Purpose of each person, place, or thing without coveting. *"Then God blessed them, and God said to them, 'Be fruitful and multiply; fill the earth and subdue it; have dominion over the fish of the sea, over the birds of the air, and over every living thing that moves on the earth.'"* Genesis 1:28.

12. Respect the Seed hidden in all things. Everything has its own place under the Sun. If we respect the process, it will respect us, causing the natural elements of life to favor us. *"And God said, 'See, I have given you every herb that yields seed which is on the face of all the earth, and every tree whose fruit yields seed; to you it shall be for food. Also, to every beast of the earth, to every bird of the air, and to everything that creeps on the earth, in which there is life, I have given every green herb for food;' and it was so."* Genesis 1:29-30.

13. Respect the Good in all things. Once we do, it becomes easier to pinpoint the win-win in all things. *"Then God saw everything that He had made, and indeed it was very good. So the evening and the morning were the sixth day."* Genesis 1:31.

14. Respect the Ending of all things. Doing so helps us to be at peace with people, places, and things that are not a part of our Divine Design or when their time is up in a particular chapter of our lives. *"Thus, the heavens and the earth, and all the host of them, were finished."* Genesis 2:1.

15. Respect the Day of Rest for all things. For we all need a day of rest and restoration, Mentally, Physically, Emotionally, Spiritually, and Relationally. *"And on the seventh day God ended His work which He had done, and He rested on the seventh day from all His work which He had done. Then God blessed the seventh day and*

sanctified it, because in it He rested from all His work which God had created and made." Genesis 2:2-3.

16. Respect the Divine History of Creation. God does not ask us to agree, but He demands Respect in this area of the Ancientness of Days and His Divine Order. *"This is the history of the heavens and the earth when they were created, in the day that the LORD God made the earth and the heavens, before any plant of the field was in the earth and before any herb of the field had grown. For the LORD God had not caused it to rain on the earth, and there was no man to till the ground; but a mist went up from the earth and watered the whole face of the ground."* Genesis 2:4-6.

17. Respect how we were created while not taking anything for granted, especially the Breath of Life. *"And the LORD God formed man of the dust of the ground, and breathed into his nostrils the breath of life; and man became a living being."* Genesis 2:7.

What does Respect have to do with our *Heavenly Perspective*? In our Heaven on Earth Experience, if we are not able to respect the simple things, we will not appreciate the Heavenly Treasures. Instead, we will find a reason to discount or second-guess the Blessings of the Kingdom.

In order to become and remain Blessed, we must first recognize that we are. If we fail to recognize this one fact, we will begin to player hate when we should be celebrating. The last thing the Kingdom wants is a party pooper raining on our parade or that of another. There is a Spiritual Calculation involved in all things, and if we fail to become grateful, we will begin to make a lot of avoidable mistakes. What does this mean? If we violate the Spiritual Calculations or the Spiritual Principles governing a person, place, or thing, we will have some form of accident or incident from within, spreading outwardly.

For example, when driving a vehicle with our natural eyes, we feel as if we are just driving, and that is it. However, from a spiritual perspective, we cannot see the behind-the-scenes calculations involved in stopping, turning, reversing, parking, driving, changing lanes, and so on. Therefore, we take this privilege for granted, becoming irresponsible in our approach. The more we disrespect the laws and the calculations associated with driving, the more we will eventually have an accident.

On the other hand, if we respect the laws and calculations, they are more apt to help us avoid having an accident or becoming a victim while working on our behalf and not against us. Let us take this a step further; humans are the only sector of Creation having this privilege. To add insult to injury, we have the nerve to become ungrateful, especially when the birds of the air are on a wing and a prayer. The beasts of the field are still on their feet, trotting to and fro, getting blisters, and searching for food with a level of uncertainty.

All in all, everything according to the Heavenly of Heavens is calculated. It does not matter if we understand it, how we feel, or what we think; the Processes of God must be respected, regardless of how they appear to our naked eyes. Once we begin to see the Kingdom differently, by Divine Default, we will begin to view people, places, and things with our Spiritual Eye or from a Heavenly Perspective.

What is the big deal about the calculations associated with our Spiritual Eye? First and foremost, according to scripture, we must understand, *"For where your treasure is, there your heart will be also."* Matthew 6:21. Secondly, *"The lamp of the body is the eye. If therefore your eye is good, your whole body will be full of light. But if your eye is bad, your whole body will be full of darkness. If therefore the light that is in you is darkness, how great is that darkness!"* Matthew 6:22-23. For this reason, Spiritual Blindness is nothing we would want to play around with. It contaminates the human psyche with the lust of the eyes, the lust of the flesh, and the pride of life through our senses, causing us to become caught up or soul-tied without us realizing we are.

As It Pleases God: Book Series

What can we do to position ourselves to develop our Spiritual Eyes, Ears, and Language from a *Heavenly Perspective?* Listed below are a few ways to do so, but not limited to such:

1. We must cease from bragging about what we do for others while expecting our Spiritual Rewards from the Kingdom. It helps us to do away with false expectations and disappointments associated with feeling used. Meanwhile, when we do whatever with no strings attached, we allow the Heavenly of Heavens to usher in the people, places, and things money cannot buy while establishing true Spiritual Value. *"Take heed that you do not do your charitable deeds before men, to be seen by them. Otherwise, you have no reward from your Father in Heaven."* Matthew 6:1.

2. We must redirect our charitable deeds as being the right thing to do, without seeking accolades from others or becoming a hypocrite behind someone's back. *"Therefore, when you do a charitable deed, do not sound a trumpet before you as the hypocrites do in the synagogues and in the streets, that they may have glory from men. Assuredly, I say to you, they have their reward."* Matthew 6:2.

3. When we decide to help someone genuinely, we do not have to seek approval from others to do the right thing proactively. We are Blessed to be a Blessing; therefore, if we allow others to judge our Blessed Provisions, we can miss the Spiritual Mark or Cue. *'But when you do a charitable deed, do not let your left hand know what your right hand is doing."* Matthew 6:3.

4. We must understand that sharing without seeking attention gives us a platform to become openly Blessed without any shame attached. *"That your charitable deed may be*

in secret; and your Father who sees in secret will Himself reward you openly. Matthew 6:4.

5. We must not seek to impress others with our ability to pray. It usually causes us to pray amiss because we are often using our personal prayers for the wrong reasons, and God weighs the heart's intent. So, we must be careful with community prayers to ensure we do not become hypocritical in our approach. *"And when you pray, you shall not be like the hypocrites. For they love to pray standing in the synagogues and on the corners of the streets, that they may be seen by men. Assuredly, I say to you, they have their reward."* Matthew 6:5.

6. We must seek to have our private time alone with God. It builds our *Spirit to Spirit* Relations and our inside voice. It helps us to recognize the Voice of God when He is speaking and how to tune out, avoid, or redirect negative chatter. *"But you, when you pray, go into your room, and when you have shut your door, pray to your Father who is in the secret place; and your Father who sees in secret will reward you openly."* Matthew 6:6.

7. We must communicate with God without saying the same thing over and over. The issues of the heart will vary, and if we are repenting about the same things, it means growth is not taking place, or we are lying to ourselves. *"And when you pray, do not use vain repetitions as the heathen do. For they think that they will be heard for their many words."* Matthew 6:7.

8. We must come clean with the issues of the heart. God knows what we are dealing with; He is waiting for us to admit, understand, and regraft it, doing our part in the process without whitewashing. *"Therefore, do not be like them. For your Father knows the things you have need of before you ask Him."* Matthew 6:8.

9. We must direct our prayers toward Heaven. If not, we subject our prayers to becoming misdirected, not knowing who we are praying to. *"In this manner, therefore, pray: Our Father in heaven, Hallowed be Your name."* Matthew 6:9.

10. We must avail ourselves to having our Heaven on Earth Experience while availing ourselves to the Will of God. We have free will to choose whether we desire a worldly or Heavenly Experience and being in the Will of God. If we do not choose, we subject ourselves to the worldly system due to our lack of clarity. *"Your kingdom come. Your will be done on earth as it is in Heaven."* Matthew 6:10.

11. We must ask for our daily bread or our portions while repenting and forgiving ourselves and others. It clears the Spiritual Channels, allowing us to receive or download from the Heavenly of Heavens. *"Give us this day our daily bread. And forgive us our debts, as we forgive our debtors."* Matthew 6:11-12.

12. We must ask for the Leading and Deliverance of the Holy Spirit to ensure we do not subject ourselves to worldly temptation designed to sift us Mentally, Physically, or Emotionally. While simultaneously redirecting all things back to the Kingdom of Heaven, securing or Spiritually Sealing our position in Christ Jesus. *"And do not lead us into temptation, but deliver us from the evil one. For Yours is the kingdom and the power and the glory forever. Amen."* Matthew 6:13.

We have all recited the Lord's Prayer without understanding the reasons behind the 'Why.' Well, today, we now know the importance of doing certain things in the Realm of the Spirit from a *Heavenly Perspective*. We can tiptoe around whatever we like, but when it comes down to the Heavenly of Heavens, we must follow Spiritual Protocol. It prevents us from being yoked, soul-tied, oppressed, or deceived because *"No one can serve two masters; for either he will hate the one and love the other, or else he will be loyal to the one and despise the other. You cannot serve God and mammon."* Matthew 6:24.

We must also keep in mind that when going about our daily duties or activities, we cannot change others. We can only change ourselves from within while impacting others outwardly. What if we have children? Here again, we must change ourselves and impact them outwardly. From a *Heavenly Perspective*, we must lead by example because children see who we are, not who we pretend to be. And they will emulate accordingly.

For example, if our children see us faking, they will learn this behavior, even if they pretend to be authentic. If we pride ourselves on being transparently authentic, becoming a work-in-progress, and solving problems in real time, they will follow suit. Yes, we must be strong for our children, but if we do not teach them how to solve issues from the inside out, they will suffer inner weaknesses, trying to appear strong.

What is the big deal, especially when we have free will to raise our children the way we like? Of course, we do have the right to do whatever we like; however, from a *Heavenly Perspective*, here is the deal: *"Every plant which My heavenly Father has not planted will be uprooted. Let them alone. They are blind leaders of the blind. And if the blind leads the blind, both will fall into a ditch."* Matthew 15:13-14. Therefore, it is always best to reel ourselves in with the Fruits of the Spirit and Christlike Character to ensure we are using and sharing them with all we come in contact with.

What if we fall short? All we need to do is identify our point of erring, repent, and self-correct. Plus, we can also repeat this scripture over and over to Spiritually Reset ourselves: *"Glory to God in the highest, and on earth peace, goodwill toward men!"* Luke 2:14. Does it work? Absolutely. The Heavenly Host used this in praising God, and if it worked for them, it would work for us in the *Fullness Therein*.

Chapter Eleven

FULLNESS THEREIN

Most often, we do not think about *Fullness* unless we are empty, and then again, once we are *Full*, we forget to give THANKS for the *Fullness Therein*, and sucker punch those who are in a state of apparent emptiness without offering a helping hand. From a Spiritual Perspective, this is a double standard.

According to the Heavenly of Heavens, the *Fullness Therein* is linked to what we have in hand with a SEED attached to it. If the Blessing or Seed becomes buried within the human psyche without any form of '*Give Back*,' we create a disservice on behalf of the Kingdom and from within, creating a symbolic form of emptiness, void, or disconnect.

Regardless of what we are doing, our condition, where we are in life, or our level of trauma, we are so Blessed beyond what we could have ever imagined in a million years. As a matter of fact, truthfully speaking, if we dare to think for a moment, God simply '*Blessed*' us to have more without us doing anything on our own accord, breaking a yoke we could not break on our own. And then, as a slap in the face to the Blesser, we have the nerve to turn up our nose at those who are where we were, develop a deaf ear to the Cycles and the Vicissitudes of Life, and think we are better or wiser than that which has already been before us. But all is not lost; the Ancient of Ancients are here to help us on our journey, giving us a Divine Understanding of the *Fullness Therein*.

What is the *Fullness Therein*? It is basically the *Fullness from Within* the Mind, Body, Soul, and Spirit, which are designed to work together as a team, building up each other. However, the moment we function on empty or with some form of disconnect, we will run out of gas, lacking the energy in that portion of ourselves. If we do not know how to shift energy positively or refuel, it will zap us, depleting the other areas that are compensating for our areas of lack.

For example, a Positive Mental Mindset compensates for us when our Body is sick, our Soul is traumatized, or our Spirit is asleep. A healthy Body will help redirect energy to the Mind when we are mentally exhausted, stimulating the Soul and awakening the Spirit. However, we are not limited to these examples, but they are a great place to start.

Once we initiate Spiritual Awareness in such a manner, the Holy Spirit will guide us the rest of the way, especially if we journal our progress. Why should we journal the prompting of the Mind, Body, Soul, and Spirit? From a Spiritual Perspective, it helps us to pinpoint imbalances, red flags, the moving of the Spirit, and the Spiritual Language of the Heavenly of Heavens. In addition, it also gives us the ability to jumpstart ourselves when we fall short, when we get zapped, or when we lower our Spiritual Guards out of outright negligence.

By mastering and charting the progress of the Mind, Body, Soul, and Spirit, we can pinpoint the areas of trouble, trauma, or zapping. How do we know if we are being zapped? We will feel the shift in our Mental Thoughts, Bodily Functions, Soulish Demeanor, or Spiritual Dormancy. A zap is similar to getting some form of small shock from an electrical device, which is not designed to hurt us, but it makes us aware of impending danger, provoking us to back up to offset further harm. To be clear, not all zaps are created equal;

therefore, we need the Holy Spirit to guide us and the Blood of Jesus to cover us amid whatever or with whomever.

As a Word to the Wise, a zapper will most often not appear as if they are going to zap us. They will come to lure us into what we like, catering to our habits, vices, or traumas, reeling us through our senses via the lust of the eyes, the lust of the flesh, and the pride of life. So, we must pay attention, becoming aware of all things appealing and unappealing alike, knowing the differences between the lesson, Blessing, testing, distraction, or outright deception. More importantly, we must become aware of positive and negative fruits and characteristics from within ourselves and others to ensure we do not get entrapped in our own nets of deceitfulness.

Picturesquely, we do not think about running out of gas from the inside out, as we go with the flow, dealing with life as it comes. Amidst all, this is what the enemy is waiting on. Our process of omission is all the enemy needs to possess us with negativity, division, chaos, and disobedience while yoking us to the core when we think we are on top of the world. When in all actuality, the world is on top of us, pressing us to the max, as the gravitational pull of life is drawing us into the Pit and spoiling our fruits. Amid our imperfections, if we fill up on the Fullness of the Kingdom and its Divine Principles, we can contend with the wiles of the enemy or the enemy from within.

Our impact in life or *Fullness Therein* depends upon us, and without 'us' and 'them,' our Heaven on Earth Experience ceases to exist; therefore, we must approach life, knowing WHO is in charge. Here is the scripture, "*Let the Heavens rejoice, and let the earth be glad; and let them say among the nations, 'The LORD reigns.' Let the sea roar, and all its fullness; let the field rejoice, and all that is in it.*" 1 Chronicles 16:31-32.

If we desire to have all God has to offer according to our Divine Blueprint, we must gain *Spirit to Spirit* access to it. What does this mean? We are all different, with a unique Spiritual Mission, having our own set of Provisions, *As It Pleases God*. Then again, we run the risk of disconnecting from the people, places, and things designed to properly equip us with the Spiritual Tools needed to complete our Purpose if we are off course.

As It Pleases God®: Book Series

What can we do to stay on course, *As It Pleases God*? It will vary from person to person; however, according to Psalm 16:5-6, we can say, "*O LORD, You are the portion of my inheritance and my cup; You maintain my lot. The lines have fallen to me in pleasant places; Yes, I have a good inheritance.*" When dealing with the '*Fullness Therein*,' reciting this positive Decree over our lives daily will help us align our Mind, Body, Soul, and Spirit with the Heavenly of Heavens. Even if we have to dial in or connect several times a day, it is well worth the effort. What makes this Decree well worth it? It will help us stay focused without being distracted by people, places, and things that have nothing to do with us or our life's direction, or wasting precious energy reacting or responding when we should be at peace.

The '*Fullness*' of the Heavenly of Heavens is nothing to play around with, especially if we lack understanding from a Kingdom Perspective. If we lack understanding, we do not know who to thank, so we ignore doing so or give it to the wrong people for all the wrong reasons, leading to idolatry. What can we do to avoid idolatrous behaviors? Listed below are a few step-by-step ways to interact with God to receive the '*Fullness Therein*,' but not limited to such, especially when it comes down to exhibiting the Fruits of the Spirit and Christlike Character:

1. '*Speak*' to Him in His Language.
2. Give '*Thanks*' to Him in all things.
3. Acknowledge His '*Goodness*.'
4. Ask and give '*Mercy*' continuously.
5. Petition for Him to '*Save Us*.'
6. Surrender to '*Gatherings*' as a team player.
7. Ask for '*Deliverance*' from ourselves and others.
8. '*Worship*' Him in Spirit and truth.
9. Understand and accept the '*Blessings*' to become a Blessing to others.
10. '*Recognize*' the signs of the time.
11. Spiritually Seal our petitions with the word, '*Amen*.'
12. Give Him the '*Praise*' for all things.

Am I pulling for straws here? Absolutely not. Therefore, let us align accordingly, *"Oh, give thanks to the LORD, for He is good! For His mercy endures forever. And say, 'Save us, O God of our salvation; gather us together, and deliver us from the Gentiles, to give thanks to Your holy name, to triumph in Your praise.' Blessed be the LORD God of Israel from everlasting to everlasting! And all the people said, 'Amen!' and praised the LORD."* 1 Chronicles 16:34-36.

How do we deal with ourselves when attempting to receive the *'Fullness Therein'* according to the Heavenly of Heavens? Listed below are a few items to help us, *As It Pleases God*, but not limited to such:

1. We must position ourselves in the Blessings of God without wallowing in the negative.
2. We must call upon the Spiritual Counsel of the Holy Spirit.
3. We must set a guard over the heart, redirecting any form of darkness into Light.
4. We must understand that the Cycle of Life will work on our behalf if we incorporate God into the equation.
5. We must know God avails, unveils, and prevails in all things in alignment with our Divine Blueprint.
6. We must position ourselves to sit on the Right Hand of God, with the Fruits of the Spirit and Christlike Character as our Platform of Righteousness.
7. We must keep ourselves in a happy state of being from the outside while rejoicing with our inner joy, intentionally spreading outwardly, and making this world a better place to live.
8. We must put the lust of the eyes, the lust of the flesh, and the pride of life under the subjection of the Holy Spirit while using the Blood of Jesus as a covering to safeguard our restful elements of hope.
9. We must avoid wayward, dubious, or destructive behaviors negatively impacting our attitude, mindset, and demeanor, spoiling our fruits and character.
10. We must live by example toward the path of righteousness, correcting the correctable in total transparency.

11. We must represent the Kingdom with our Heaven on Earth Experience.
12. We must be willing to live the Good Life while showing others how to do likewise, with lasting benefits, keeping our Bloodline engulfed with Divine Provisions of the Kingdom.

According to the Heavenly of Heavens, if we take one step at a time, we can overcome anything; however, before we move on, for the above instructions, here is the scripture: *"I will bless the LORD who has given me counsel; my heart also instructs me in the night seasons. I have set the LORD always before me; because He is at my right hand I shall not be moved. Therefore, my heart is glad, and my glory rejoices; my flesh also will rest in hope. For You will not leave my soul in Sheol, nor will You allow Your Holy One to see corruption. You will show me the path of life; in Your presence is fullness of joy; at Your right hand are pleasures forevermore."* Psalm 16:7-11.

One would ask, 'Where am I getting this information from?' In order to receive the Fullness of my Giftings according to my Divine Blueprint, these are my notes from the Bible and the Spiritual Utterances from my *Spirit to Spirit* Connection with my Heavenly Father. As my *Give-Back* to the Kingdom, I share the information, *As It Pleases God*, helping others to do likewise, Spiritually Seeing, Hearing, and Speaking according to their Divine Blueprint. As a result, bringing them in Purpose on purpose with an understanding of their *What, When, Where, Why, How,* and with *Whom* Spiritual Truths.

According to the Heavenly of Heavens, there is Hidden Wisdom in all things, especially in scripture, making it befitting to our situation, understanding, or Kingdom Revelation, *As It Pleases God*. All we need to do is make use of it, *As It Pleases Him*, but no worries, the next chapter will share how to maximize this process from His Divine Perspective.

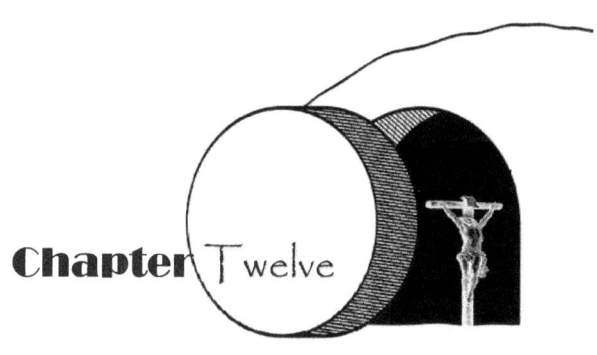

Chapter Twelve

AS IT PLEASES GOD

*A*s *It Pleases God*, timing is everything! In the Kingdom, if we move at the wrong time, we become unsynchronized. So, we must continue to realign ourselves accordingly, calibrating our Spiritual Senses on a moment-by-moment basis. For this reason, we must understand the differences in the worldly and Godly systems embedded *In Him*. If not, we can become swept away by our senses, habits, and lusts.

When our timing is off, we are often faced with self-pleasing and people-pleasing, but if we dare to gather the courage to become a God Pleaser, *As It Pleases Him*, our lives will change beyond what we could ever imagine. We would not have to run behind Him in doing so; all we need to do is avail ourselves to His Will and Ways, and He will come to us, hook, line, and sinker, availing Himself to us. Blasphemy, right? Wrong. *"Whoever has my commands and keeps them is the one who loves me. The one who loves me will be loved by my Father, and I too will love them and show myself to them."* John 14:21.

We often confuse the Weapon of Confidence with pompousness, whereas Spiritual Confidence rests in a knowing without playing pretend. What if someone is pressuring us to become someone we are not? Once we know 'Who' we are and 'Why' we are, it relieves the pressure. How is this possible? The only time we experience pressure is when we are unsure, fearful, masking something, harboring negativity, or trying to convince someone. If we have a desire to come boldly to the Throne of God, *Spirit to Spirit*, without having peer pressure and *As It Pleases God*, we must keep this in mind: *"Owe no one anything except to love one another, for he who loves another has fulfilled the law."* Romans 13:8.

Our healing, cure, therapy, medicine, or the antidote we are looking for, *As It Pleases God*, is ANCIENT. How is this possible, especially when living in the now? Suppose we desire a Spiritual Healing from the inside out, similar to our Forefathers, *As It Pleases God*. In this case, we must glean from their personable mistakes and experiences to maximize our present moment. For example, if we want to become more like Jesus, we must emulate His life, bringing His characteristics from the past to the present.

On the other hand, if we want to avoid someone's mistakes, we must avoid their past behaviors to ensure they do not affect or hinder us. How can we make this make sense, especially when using Ancient Principles in our present reality? For example, the Book of Judges 13-16 shares the story of Samson, exposing his strengths and weaknesses to help us avoid making the same mistakes.

Plus, it shows us what will happen if we let our guard down in a moment of Mental, Physical, Emotional, or Spiritual weakness or if we succumb to disobedience, especially when we have been Spiritually Marked, Warned, and Anointed. Then again, when we know beyond a shadow of a doubt that our strength and courage are coming from God Almighty, and we allow the lusts of the eye, the lust of the flesh, and the pride of life to take us down, causing us to get our eyes gouged and having to tread the mill, we cannot lay the blame elsewhere.

We can put a new spin on whatever we like and downplay the Ancient of Ancients, but according to scripture, there is nothing new under the sun. We just have different characters with an up-to-date plot with people like us. Is this Biblical? *"That which has been is what will be, that which is done is what will be done, and there is nothing new under the sun. Is there anything of which it may be said, See, this is new? It has already been in ancient times before us."* Ecclesiastes 1:9-10.

I know we are up-to-date with all of the latest gadgets and technology, and the things of old seem to be a little dated; however, we are so insecure and lost beyond what we could ever imagine. According to the Heavenly of Heavens, our inner man has an unfulfilled longing for Spirituality, which we do not have a clue about tapping into without God Almighty. As a result, we turn to Social Media to fill in the void, only to find it is leading us into the Pit without knowing why. Consequently, we use pompousness as a superficial form of courage instead of using humility as Spiritual Leverage, *As It Pleases God*.

When it comes down to *Pleasing God*, it is not predicated on what is TRENDING. It is established based on the contents of our heart posture. The moment we find ourselves questioning God about the 'show me, show me' in our lives, we already know something is not lining up Spiritually. I often find those who ask for a sign when they already know something is not right! From my perspective, they should be asking for a CONFIRMATION of what they are feeling.

Now, the question is, 'Is the SIGN and CONFIRMATION the same?' The answer is, 'No.' When ASKING for a sign, it is usually derived from a place of doubt, and confirmation is from a place of knowing.

On the other hand, if we have never placed a request or asked a question, and God sends the information to provoke our awareness to protect us, to guide us, or as a covenant—this is indeed a SIGN. Pictorially, this is similar to when God sent the Rainbow as a covenant. Here is the scripture, *"I have set my rainbow in the clouds, and it will be the sign of the covenant between me and the earth. Whenever I bring clouds over the earth, and the rainbow appears in the clouds, I will remember my covenant between you and me and all living creatures of every kind. Never again will the waters become a flood to destroy all life. Whenever the rainbow appears in the clouds, I will see it and remember the everlasting covenant between God and all living creatures of every kind on the earth. So, God said to Noah, This is the sign of the covenant I have established between me and all life on the earth."* Genesis 9:13-17.

How does God send signs to us? It is not limited to one way; He can use the Holy Spirit, a person, a dream, a place, an animal, a conversation, an image, etc. We cannot limit God, nor should we limit the sign. Our responsibility is to CONFIRM the Source even if we are or are not well-versed in doing so.

Here is the scripture to confirm the trying of the Spirit, *"Beloved, believe not every spirit, but try the spirits whether they are of God: because many false prophets are gone out into the world."* 1 John 4:1. How do we go about doing so? In this instance, we should try the Spirit by asking for confirmation to validate if it is coming from the correct Source by using the Bible. We can also align it with the Fruits of the Spirit, and so on. Here again, we cannot limit God.

By NOT knowing the difference between the Sign and Confirmation, we will make vital mistakes Spiritually, causing Spiritual Blindness, Deafness, and Muteness. Listen, misconstrued instructions have been our ultimate downfall since the Garden of Eden in Genesis 3. The Deception in the Garden has created a domino effect on our lives; as a result, God will PLACE or HIDE the information in our hearts through our instincts, senses, and conscience to calibrate our discernment faculties, *As It Pleases Him.*

In turn, this gives us the ability to invoke the Holy Spirit for Divine Guidance, apply scripture, and do our homework to make sure what we are doing or what is being done aligns with Godly Character, Divine Instructions, or Spiritual Protocol. More importantly, we need to know this: *"When he brings out his own sheep, he goes before them; and the sheep follow him, for they know his voice. Yet they will by no means follow a stranger, but will flee from him, for they do not know the voice of strangers."* John 10:4-5. *"I am the good shepherd, and I know My sheep, and am known by My own."* John 10:14.

Can the Bible really provide Divine Confirmation? Absolutely! The Word of God is the Gateway to the Kingdom. Here is the secret to this matter: If we are going to use the Bible, we cannot use it without God, period. If we use one without the other, we set ourselves up for destruction due to a Spiritual Violation of Spiritual Order. We need His Principles to please Him, we need Him to carry out His Word through the Holy Spirit, and we need the Blood of Jesus as our Sacrificial Lamb. Why is this the case? Here is another secret: Satan knows the Word of God, Spiritual Order, and His Principles better than most Believers. So, why would we attempt to contend with Spiritual Principalities we do not understand without God Almighty? Wait, wait, wait, do not answer this question yet. Let us go deeper since this is the last chapter in this book.

Satan's ultimate goal is to use the Bible against us to keep the dots from connecting in our lives, *As It Pleases God*, especially if we are oblivious to Spiritual Protocol or if we are out of a relationship with God. Remember, he sat with God in the Heavens, so he knows what to do to keep us distracted, and he knows what to do to keep us in a Spiritual Violation zone with our character traits, lusts, habits, and negativity. Listen, his goal is to keep us from knowing the truth about using the Word and the Spirit of God while covering ourselves with the Blood of Jesus.

The moment we try to alter our lives or the lives of others that violate the Will of God, the will of an individual, or without God's Absolute Sovereignty, we get in trouble Spiritually. As a result, this person will curse their own hands or create generational curses for stepping into a Realm of the Spirit unequipped, out of order, with the wrong character traits, with ulterior motives, with coveting, or with unjustifiable waywardness.

For example, we would never walk into a Judge's Courtroom exhibiting such disorderly behavior or disrespect towards them. If we do, we will have ourselves thrown into jail so fast that it will make our heads spin without a jury.

To take this a step further, this sort of behavior reminded me of Moses when he struck the rock twice with his staff in Numbers 20. As a result, he was punished by God, and he was not allowed to enter the Promised Land due to his lack of trust, his uncontrollable anger, his disobedience, as well as his self-righteous ability to idolize himself, as opposed to acknowledging that it is God working through him to bring forth such miracles.

Our *Spirit to Spirit* Relationship must become equipped with more listening to God than talking. If we talk to God more than we listen, there is a disconnect somewhere. In my opinion, if we have too much chatter physically, it blocks our Spiritual Ears from hearing what needs to be heard.

How do we know if we have too much chatter going on? The best way to evaluate the mental chatter is to find a quiet space alone to meditate or to just sit in total silence. If our mind is all over the place negatively, or we cannot sit still as our mind bounces all over the place, this is an indication of too much chatter or an overzealous amount of distractions.

The stillness of ourselves from the inside out provides a means of withdrawing from the busyness of life. In the Eye of God, if we are able to purge the chatter or negativity Mentally, Physically, and Emotionally, we are better able to focus or connect *Spirit to Spirit*, gaining Spiritual Insight, *As It Pleases Him*.

When making willing attempts to do right or get something right, *As It Pleases God*, the Heavenly of Heavens honors it, more so than those who are complacent. Simply put, He wants us to work on ourselves, *As It Pleases Him*, and Spiritually Till our own ground. Nevertheless, here are six reasons why, but not limited to such:

1. God wants us to be PRODUCTIVE.
2. God wants us to INCREASE and be FRUITFUL.
3. God wants us to REPRODUCE and MULTIPLY.
4. God wants us to GIVE.
5. God wants us to GROW.
6. God wants us to be THANKFUL.
7. God wants us to LOVE.
8. God wants us to OVERCOME.
9. God wants us to TAKE RESPONSIBILITY.
10. God wants us to PLEASE HIM.
11. God wants us to TRUST HIM.
12. God wants us to use our SPIRITUAL TOOLS.

In conclusion, you have what it takes to succeed on any level and to rise to any occasion. The key to unlocking this potential lies in believing in yourself humbly and recognizing the Divine Greatness that resides within your loins. In the same way that seeds hold the potential to grow into magnificent trees, you too, as a Spiritual Being having a human experience, have the same potential. You, as the Tree of Life in the Eye of God, contain the same capacity and power to blossom if you nurture your seeds, dreams, thoughts, and desires, *As It Pleases Him*. As I have Divinely Poured into you, do likewise, while Spiritually Tilling your own ground with self-improvement and personal development.

In tandem with this better version of yourself through Divine Cultivation, you must also engage in positively working on yourself daily to become better, stronger, and wiser, *As It Pleases God*, with a work-in-progress mindset, and for the Greater Good of mankind. Spirit to Spirit, here is the Spiritual Seal I want to leave with you: *"For if you truly amend your ways and your deeds, if you truly practice justice between a man and his neighbor, If you oppress not the stranger, the fatherless, and the widow, and shed not innocent blood in this place, neither walk after other gods to your hurt: Then will I cause you to dwell in this place, in the land that I gave to your fathers, forever and ever."* Jeremiah 7:5-7. From me to you, as The Why Doctor sent from the Heavenly of Heavens, Grow Great, and Many Blessings to all.

Dr. Y. Bur

www.ingramcontent.com/pod-product-compliance
Lightning Source LLC
Chambersburg PA
CBHW071449160426
43195CB00013B/2059